THE
GOOD
GOOD
PIG

BALLANTINE BOOKS
NEW YORK

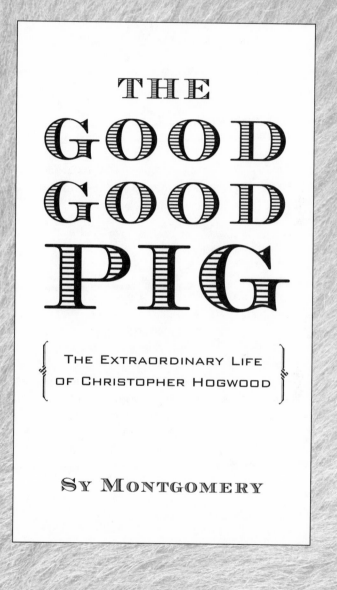

THE
GOOD
GOOD
PIG

{ THE EXTRAORDINARY LIFE
OF CHRISTOPHER HOGWOOD }

SY MONTGOMERY

Published in the United States by Ballantine Books, an imprint of
The Random House Publishing Group, a division of
Random House, Inc., New York.

BALLANTINE and colophon are registered trademarks of
Random House, Inc.

Library of Congress Cataloging-in-Publication Data
Montgomery, Sy.
The good good pig : the extraordinary life of Christopher Hogwood /
Sy Montgomery.
p.   cm.
ISBN 0-345-48137-2
1. Swine as pets—New Hampshire—Anecdotes. 2. Montgomery, Sy.
3. Pet owners—New Hampshire—Biography. 4. Human-animal
relationships—New Hampshire—Anecdotes. I. Title.
SF395.6.M66 2006
636.4'0887—dc22   2005057094

Printed in the United States of America on acid-free paper

www.ballantinebooks.com

2   4   6   8   9   7   5   3   1

First Edition

Book design by Susan Turner

To Kate, Jane, and Lilla Cabot

Contents

THE
GOOD
GOOD
PIG

CHAPTER 1
RUNTHOOD

CHRISTOPHER HOGWOOD CAME HOME ON MY LAP IN A SHOE BOX.

On a rain-drenched April evening, so cold the frogs were silent, so gray we could hardly see our barn, my husband drove our rusting Subaru over mud roads sodden with melted snow. Pig manure caked on our boots. The smell of a sick animal hung heavy in our clothes.

It did not seem an auspicious time to make the life-changing choice of adopting a pig.

That whole spring, in fact, had been terrible. My father, an Army general, a hero I so adored that I had confessed in Sunday school that I loved him more than Jesus, was dying painfully, gruesomely of lung cancer. He had survived the Bataan Death March. He had survived three years of Japanese prison camps. In the last months of my father's life, my glamorous, slender mother—still as crazy about him as the day they'd met forty years before—resisted getting a chairlift, a wheelchair, a hospice nurse. She believed he could survive anything. But he could not survive this.

The only child, I had flown back and forth from New Hampshire to Virginia to be with my parents whenever I could. I would return to New Hampshire from these wrenching trips to try to finish my first book, a tribute to my heroines, primatologists Jane Goodall, Dian Fossey, and Biruté Galdikas. The research had been challenging: I had been charged by an angry silverback gorilla in Zaire, stood up by Jane Goodall in Tanzania, undressed by an orangutan in Borneo, and accosted for money by a gun-toting guard ten thousand feet up the side of a volcano in Rwanda. Now I was on a tight deadline, and the words wouldn't come.

My husband, who writes on American history and preservation, was in the heat of writing his second book. *In the Memory House* is about time and change in New England, set largely in our corner of the world. But it looked like it might not stay ours for long. For the past three years, ever since our marriage, we had lived, first as renters and then as caretakers, in an idyllic, 110-year-old white clapboard farmhouse on eight acres in southern New Hampshire, near mountains that Thoreau had climbed. Ours was the newest house in our small neighborhood. Though our neighbors owned the two-hundred-year-old "antiques" that real estate agents praised, this place had everything I'd ever wanted: a fenced pasture, a wooded brook, a three-level barn, and forty-year-old lilacs framing the front door. But it was about to be sold out from under us. Our landlords, writer-artist friends our age whose parents had bankrolled the house, had moved to Paris and didn't plan to come back. We were desperate to buy the place.

But because we were both freelance writers, our income was deemed too erratic to merit the mortgage.

It seemed I was about to lose my father, my book, and my home.

But for Christopher Hogwood, the spring had been more terrible yet.

HE HAD BEEN BORN IN MID-FEBRUARY, ON A FARM OWNED BY George and Mary Iselin, about a thirty-five-minute drive from our house. We knew George and Mary by way of my best friend, Gretchen Vogel. Gretchen knew we had a lot in common. "You'll love them," Gretchen had assured me. "They have pigs!"

In fact, George had been raising pigs longer than Mary had known him. "If you're a farmer or a hippie," George had reasoned, "you can make money raising pigs." George and Mary were quintessential hippie farmers: born, as we were, in the 1950s, they lived the ideals of the late '60s and early '70s— peace, joy, and love—and, both blessed with radiant blue eyes, blond hair, and good looks, always looked like they had just woken up refreshed from sleeping in a pile of leaves somewhere, perhaps with elves in attendance. They were dedicated back-to-the-landers who lived out of their garden and made their own mayonnaise out of eggs from their free-range hens. They were idealistic, but resourceful, too: it did not escape them that there are vast quantities of free pig food out there, from bakeries, school cafeterias, grocery stores, and factory outlets. George and Mary would get a call to come pick up forty pounds of potato chips or a truckload of Twinkies. To their dismay, they discovered their kids, raised on homemade, organic meals, would sometimes sneak down to the barn at 4 a.m. and eat the junk food they got for the pigs. ("We found out because in the morning we'd find these chocolate rings around their mouths," Mary told me.)

On their shaggy, overgrown 165 acres, they cut their own firewood, hayed the fields, and raised not only pigs but draft horses, rabbits, ducks, chickens, goats, sheep, and children. But the pigs, I suspect, were George's favorites. And they were mine, too.

We visited them every spring. We didn't get to see George and Mary often—our schedules and lives were so different— but the baby pigs ensured we never lost touch. The last time we'd visited was the previous March, at the close of sugaring season, when George was out boiling sap from their sugar maples. March in New Hampshire is the dawn of mud season, and the place looked particularly disheveled. Rusting farm machinery sat stalled, in various states of repair and disrepair, among the mud and wire fencing and melting snow. Colorful, fraying laundry was strung across the front porch like Tibetan prayer flags. Inside the house, an old cottage in desperate need of paint, the floors were coming up and the ceilings were coming down. Late that morning, in a kitchen steamy from the kettle boiling on the woodstove, we found a seemingly un- countable number of small children in flannel pajamas—their three kids plus a number of cousins and visiting friends— sprawled across plates of unfinished pancakes or crawling stickily across the floor. The sink was piled with dirty dishes. As Mary reached for a mug from the pile, she mentioned every- one was just getting over the flu. Would we like a cup of tea?

No thanks, Howard and I answered hastily—but we would like to see the pigs again.

The barn was not Norman Rockwell. It was more like Norman Rockwell meets Edward Hopper. The siding was an- cient, the sills rotting, the interior cavernous and furry with cobwebs. We loved it. We would peer over the tall stall doors, our eyes adjusting to the gloom, and find the stalls with piglets in residence. Once we had located a family, we would climb in and play with them.

On some farms, this would be a dangerous proposition. Sows can weigh over five hundred pounds and can snap if they feel their piglets are threatened. The massive jaws can effortlessly crush a peach pit—or a kneecap. The razor-sharp canines strop each other. And for good reason: in the wild, pigs need to be strong and brave. In his hunting days in Brazil, President Theodore Roosevelt once saw a jaguar dismembered by South American native pigs. Although pigs are generally good-natured, more people are killed each year by pigs than by sharks. (Which should be no surprise—how often do you get to see a shark?) Pigs raised on crowded factory farms, tortured into insanity, have been known to eat anything that falls into the pigpen, including the occasional child whose parents are foolish enough to let their kid wander into such a place unsupervised. Feral pigs (of which there are more than four million running around in the United States alone) can kill adult humans if they are threatened. That pigs occasionally eat people has always struck me as only fair, considering the far vaster number of pigs eaten by humans.

But George's sows were all sweethearts. When we entered a stall, the sow, lying on her side to facilitate nursing, would usually raise her giant, 150-pound head, cast us a benign glance from one intelligent, lash-fringed eye, flex her wondrous and wet nose disk to capture our scent, and utter a grunt of greeting. The piglets were adorable miniatures of their behemoth parents—some pink, some black, some red, some spotted, and some with handsome racing stripes, like baby wild boars, looking like very large chipmunks. At first the piglets seemed unsure whether they should try to eat us or run away. They would rush at us in a herd, squealing, then race back on tiny, high-heeled hooves to their giant, supine mother for another tug on her milky teats. And then they would charge forth again, growing bold enough to chew on shoes or untie laces. Many of the folks who bought a pig from George would later make a point of telling him what a great pig it was. Even though the babies were almost all destined for the freezer, the folks who bought them seldom mentioned what these pigs tasted like as hams or chops or sausage. No, the people would always comment that George's were particularly *nice* pigs.

The year Chris was born was a record one for piglets. Because we were beset and frantic, we didn't visit the barn that February or March. But that year, unknown to us, George and Mary had twenty sows—more than ever before—and almost all of them had record litters.

"Usually a sow doesn't want to raise more than ten piglets," Mary explained to me. "Usually a sow has ten good working teats." (They actually have twelve, but only ten are usually in working order.) When a sow has more than ten piglets, somebody is going to lose out—and that somebody is the runt.

A runt is distinguished not only by its small size and helpless predicament. Unless pulled from the litter and nursed by people, a runt is usually doomed, for it is a threat to the entire pig family. "A runt will make this awful sound—*Nynh! Nynh! Nynh!*" Mary told me. "It's just awful. It would attract predators. So the sow's response is often to bite the runt in half, to stop the noise. But sometimes she can't tell who's doing it. She might bite a healthy one, or trample some of the others trying to get to the runt. It isn't her fault, and you can't blame her. It screws up the whole litter."

Every year on the farm, there was a runt or two. George would usually remove the little fellow and bottle-feed it goat milk in the house. With such personalized care, the runt will usually survive. But the class of 1990, with more than two hundred piglets, had no fewer than eighteen runts—so many that George and Mary had to establish a "runt stall" in the barn.

Christopher Hogwood was a runt among runts. He was the smallest of them all—half the size of the other runts. He is a particularly endearing piglet, Mary told us, with enormous ears and black and white spots, and a black patch over one eye like Spuds McKenzie, the bull terrier in the beer commercial. But Mary was convinced he would never survive. It would be more humane to kill him, she urged, than to let him suffer. But George said—as he often does—"Where there's life, there's hope." The little piglet hung on.

But he didn't grow.

Because intestinal worms are common in pigs, George and Mary dosed the piglets with medicine to kill the parasites—and perhaps boost the runt's growth. "The wormer didn't do a thing for him," Mary told us. "He probably had a touch of every disease in the barn—he had worms, he had erysipelas, he had rhinopneumonitis—and yet he wouldn't die. He just wouldn't!"

They called him the Spotted Thing. Though he didn't die, it was unlikely anyone would buy him. Folks usually buy a pig in April to raise for the freezer, when the piglets typically weigh fifty to sixty-five pounds. Christopher weighed about seven.

Mary kept telling George, "You've got to kill that piglet." George would take him out to the manure pile, intending to dispatch him quickly with a blow to the head from his shovel. But George would watch the little piglet—his soulful eyes, his big floppy ears, his admirable will to live—and just couldn't do it. "I must have sent him out to kill that piglet fifteen times," Mary remembered. Finally George refused to even go out there. "*You* kill the piglet!" he said to his wife.

Mary took the spotted runt out to the manure pile with the shovel. She couldn't do it, either.

That's when she called my husband, Howard. I was in Virginia.

"I can't believe I'm going to make this offer to ruin your life," Mary began. Would we take the sick piglet?

Howard was constantly battling my efforts to stock the house with various orphaned animals. He would not let me enter the local humane shelter. We had already adopted a neglected cockatiel and an about-to-be-homeless crimson rosella parrot. When our landlords moved to Paris, we adopted their loving gray and white cat, Mika, who followed Howard and me on walks like a dog and came when we called her. We also had had two peach-faced lovebirds once, but now we were down to one. When things went wrong with our animals, it usually happened when I was away. On a morning earlier that year, one of the times I was in Virginia caring for my dad, Howard found the male lovebird, Gladstone, on the bottom of the cage, which is a bad enough sign, but on closer inspection, Howard saw that his head was missing. The female, Peapack, sat unperturbed on her perch. We renamed the female Tonton Macoute.

My frequent travels—sometimes I was gone for months, disappearing into some jungle, researching stories for newspapers and magazines and books—were among the reasons Howard wanted no more animals. Once I had gone to Australia to live in a tent in the outback for half a year to study emus. When I'd left, we had five pet ferrets. When I came back, there were eighteen of them—and the babies all bit viciously until I tamed them by carrying them around constantly next to my skin, under my shirt (giving new meaning to the term "hair shirt"). Howard, understandably, did not want to get stuck caring for an arkload of creatures who would surely choose my next absence to run amok, overpopulate, or decapitate one another.

"Normally I wouldn't even give her the message," Howard told Mary. "But her father's dying, and this might be a good idea."

HOWARD KNEW THAT IF ANYTHING COULD SOOTHE MY SOUL, IT would be an animal. I always feel better in the company of animals; I am drawn to them so strongly it leaves some people alarmed. Once I leaped out of a moving truck in India in order to stroke a nine-foot-long wild python. (As my fellow travelers in the truck stared in horror, I petted the snake's tail while it turned its head to look at me benignly.)

A number of my friends have suggested, not always jokingly, I might be half animal myself. In my travels around the world, it appears that others see this too: shamans and fortune-tellers have told me again and again I am a very old soul—but that this is my first incarnation as a human.

That feels true. I've always known I am different. At times that has made me feel shy and awkward among other people, as if they were looking at me funny. (Possibly because the cockatiel who sat on my head as I worked left droppings in my hair.) But I am different inside, too. While other people are thinking about a new kitchen or a Caribbean cruise, or whether their child will win the soccer match, or what to wear to a party, I am thinking about how a possum's tail feels as it grips a branch, or whether the snapping turtle who tried to lay eggs in our yard last year will come back this fall.

Like a not-quite-human creature living among people far more comfortable in their own skins, I always felt a gap between me and more "normal" people. But, though neither Howard nor I realized it at the time, in the shoe box on my lap that gray spring day, we carried a creature who would bridge that gap in a way I'd never before dreamed possible. Because Christopher Hogwood would prove, in many ways, to be more human than I am.

WHAT WOULD WE DO WITH A PIG? PEOPLE WANTED TO KNOW. He was certainly not for the freezer, we would quickly assure them. I am a vegetarian and Howard is Jewish.

Of course we loved pigs—but who doesn't? After all, what is more jolly and uplifting than a pig? Everything about a pig makes people want to laugh out loud with joy: the way their lardy bulk can mince along gracefully on tiptoe hooves, the way their tails curl, their unlikely, but extremely useful, flexible nose disks, their great, greedy delight in eating. But we knew precious little about them.

When I was six, visiting my mother's mother in Arkansas, I had spent a blissful afternoon with a little boy hanging around his father's pigsty. The pigs were huge and pink and made fabulous, expressive noises. I was fascinated. I apparently classed them with horses (not a bad guess, as both are hoofed mammals—but new DNA evidence shows horses are actually more closely related evolutionarily to dogs than to pigs) because I almost immediately got on the back of one of them as if she were a pony. The pig generously let me ride around on her. This was much talked about in the dusty little cotton-growing town of Lexa, where my glamorous mother had, improbably, grown up—a place where nothing much more exciting than this ever happens. Later, the boy named a pig after me. I relished this honor so much that even though I never saw the boy again, I recall his name to this day—as he surely recalls mine, more than four decades later, having said it daily over the life of his pig.

Since then, my experience with pigs was limited to visits to George and Mary's, the hog pens at local agricultural fairs, and a single meeting with our neighbor's huge brown boar, Ben. All too soon after our meeting, though, Ben disappeared into the neighbor's freezer.

But my husband seemed ready to embrace this new member of the family. Howard had already selected a new name for the Spotted Thing. He would be named in honor of an exponent of early music. The original Christopher Hogwood is a conductor and musicologist, and founder of the Academy of Ancient Music. We often used to write while listening to his conducted work on National Public Radio. So Christopher Hogwood was an apt name for several reasons. Pigs' affinity for classical music is well known; many an old-time hog farmer piped it into the sty to keep the pigs calm. As Howard likes to say, what earlier music is there than a pig's grunting?

But Christopher Hogwood did not grunt that first night. His breathing was wet and noisy. His eyes were runny, and so was his other end. We had no pig medicine. We didn't even have a proper sty. We didn't know how long he'd live. We didn't know how big he'd get. We didn't have a clue what we were getting into.

How long *do* pigs live? This was a question we would often be asked, and our answer always shocked everyone: six months. Most pigs are raised for slaughter, and this happens quite literally at a tender age, once they reach about 250 pounds. A few lucky sows and breeder boars will be allowed to live for years, but they, too, are usually dispatched when their productivity wanes. Even breeder boars seldom live past 6 or 7, because they become so heavy they would crush the young sows who produce the biggest litters.

Relatively few people keep pigs as pets. Those who do usually keep Vietnamese potbellied pigs. Vietnam, with a porcine population of about 11.6 million (winning top honors for most pigs in Southeast Asia), manages to cram so many pigs into such a small area by breeding extraordinarily small pigs—but *small* is a relative term when it comes to swine. Vietnamese potbellied pigs, if allowed to live to maturity at about age five, typically grow to about 150 pounds. From Vietnamese potbellied stock, scientists have bred even smaller pigs for research purposes—"micropigs" who might weigh as little as thirty pounds and stand only fourteen inches tall, and who can make fine pets. But many pigs touted as tiny turn out to be of mixed porcine parentage and, to their owners' horror, quickly outgrow their miniature dimensions, necessitating potbelly rescue groups such as Pigs Without Partners (Los Angeles) or L'il Orphan Hammies (in Solvang, California). Even the ones who stay small can mean big problems. One woman we know had to give away her Vietnamese potbelly because he would bite whenever he thought that she or her husband were taking up too much space in their communal bed.

Christopher Hogwood was no Vietnamese potbelly, but there was a decent chance, Mary promised us, that he would stay small. That first night, we couldn't picture him growing much bigger than the shoe box in which we carried his shivering, emaciated form. We couldn't see that far ahead—and I didn't want to. That spring, it seemed I woke every day to sorrow, as every day carried me closer to my father's death.

I could barely allow myself to hope Christopher would survive the night.

CHAPTER 2

**BUYING
THE FARM**

FOR SO LONG, EACH MORNING HAD FELT THE SAME. FROM SLEEP, consciousness came on like a slow sickness. For a moment I would wonder vaguely what was wrong. Then it would hit me—my father's cancer, the looming deadline for the book, the home we were going to lose—and I would lie still as if pinned by its weight. "*Now* what?" I would think. I didn't want to get up.

Until the morning I woke up and remembered a baby pig was in the barn.

Originally I had envisioned him sleeping with us, in the bed. Howard, possibly influenced by the leaky state of the sick pig's rear end, had vetoed the idea. Chris should not be raised as a house pig, he insisted. My housekeeping was bad enough as it was.

So that first night, Christopher Hogwood was exiled to the ground floor of the barn. We had prepared a cozy nest. There were no stalls in the barn, but no matter: among the charms of an old barn is a vast archive of farm and garden implements as well as leftover building materials and fencing supplies, the inherited riches of a century of previous owners and their animals. Our landlord's three-level barn, for instance, contained, among other things, a trove of New Hampshire license plates from different eras, an ancient wagon wheel, a granite millstone, a lead-lined grain bin, windows, doors, and screens of various sizes, rolls of chicken and turkey wire, a pile of wooden loading pallets, a jumble of metal fence stakes, a 1980s *Gone with the Wind* poster parody (Margaret Thatcher in the arms of Ronald Reagan), a framed print of the *Mona Lisa,* and a boat toilet. From such a collection you can usually find, if not the very thing you want, at least something that will do.

Gretchen had come over to help us with the pig nursery. Raising organic vegetables, Siamese cats, and Connemara ponies on a hardscrabble farm in the next town over, she was an expert at making do: she had obtained the foam mattress for her bed from the dump ("*before* it had been rained on," she boasted). The stone foundation of the barn would serve as one outside wall, and two old doors, set on their sides and propped up with concrete blocks, created temporary back and side walls. Although the lower level of the barn had a huge sliding door on rollers, the bottom had rotted out, and a piglet could easily crawl beneath it to escape. But Gretchen saw instantly how to proceed. In front of our temporary pen, she placed a two-by-four on its long side, into which, incredibly, precisely fitted the slats of one of the wooden pallets. Voilà: half a fence-like wall, about three feet high. Another pallet, tied with string to one of the barn's wooden beams, created the other half, forming a gate we could swing open.

On the barn's dirt floor we had scattered two bales of clean, fragrant wood shavings. We made a bed from a couple of flakes of sweet hay. Here, on that first night, as I knelt beside him stroking and kissing his stunted, spotted form, Christopher Hogwood pushed his nose disk beneath the hay, tucked his hooves beneath him, and went almost immediately to sleep.

Still, I had worried about him all night. What if he got sicker? Could we pay extensive vet bills on top of the airfares to Virginia? Or worse—what if I found his little body lifeless in the hay? I rushed out of the house still in my nightshirt to see him. Already, I realized, I loved him so much it scared me.

ANIMALS HAVE ALWAYS BEEN MY REFUGE, MY AVATARS, MY SPIRIT twins. As soon as I learned to talk, I began to inform people I was actually a dog. Next, for an entire year, I insisted I was a horse. My father obliged by calling me "Pony," taking me on endless pony rides, and patiently staring with me for hours at every animal in the zoo. The hippo, whose pen I toddled into at the zoo in Frankfurt, Germany, before I was two, failed to trample or bite me, instead behaving like most of the animals I met—as if I belonged with them. Dragonflies, butterflies, and wild birds would light on my shoulders. Beetles and spiders were welcome to crawl on my skin. I preferred their company to that of other children, whom I found noisy and erratic.

When I was old enough to think about it, I realized I understood animals in a different way than other people, probably because I had the patience to watch them and see how interesting and compelling they really are. Perhaps animals revealed themselves to me because I didn't wiggle and scream like other kids. Other parents were astonished to find I had sat still long enough for artists to complete two portraits of me before I was three—paintings showing an infant, and then a toddler, with an unusually intense, focused gaze. Motionless and silent for hours, I was watching the flame of a lit candle.

My father was proud of my concentration. My mother feared I was retarded. Her worries deepened when I was sent home on my first day of kindergarten for biting a little boy after he tore the legs off a daddy longlegs. Even then I knew: the daddy longlegs and his kin were my tribe; the cruel little boy was not.

It was not that I disliked people; some of them were interesting and kind. But even the nice ones were no more compelling or important to me than other creatures. Then, as now, to me humans are but one species among billions of other equally vivid and thrilling lives. I was never drawn to other children simply because they were human. Humans seemed to me a rather bullying species, and I was on the side of the underdog.

Still, my mother cherished hopes I would turn out like a normal child. She bought me baby dolls. I flung them aside. But first I would strip off their clothes and use them to lovingly dress the stuffed baby caimans my father had brought back from South America. I would sometimes emerge from my room pushing a doll's pram, displaying the toothy, dressed-up reptiles to the horrified wives of colonels and generals gathered for my mother's bridge and cocktail parties.

This wasn't the sort of daughter my poor mother had in mind. On her Singer Featherweight, she sewed elaborate, frilly dresses to go with the lacy little girls' socks and patent leather shoes she bought at the PX. For her husband's promotion to brigadier general, a ceremony at which he also took command of the Brooklyn Army Terminal, she dressed up her blond six-year-old like those baby dolls I had flung aside, complete with bonnet and little white gloves. I remember wishing I were wearing fatigues and combat boots like the other soldiers.

After all, hadn't I helped my father get his general's stars? Every night, before his promotion, we had a ritual: I would ride on his shoulders as he walked the green border of the oriental rug, pretending I was a circus girl and he was a giant gorilla walking a tightrope over a pit of snakes. He was teaching me to be brave, to fear nothing, to hunger for wild experiences. We were practicing, I believed, for adventures we would one day have together. We would explore the world—Africa, where the real gorillas were, and Australia, where strange and alluring pouched mammals such as kangaroos and koalas lived. But first, I would need to grow up, and he would need to trade the eagles on his shoulders for a brigadier's stars. So each night, before bed, I would seize the moon and the stars from the sky and put them in the pocket of my father's uniform, and kiss him goodnight.

FINDING CHRISTOPHER ALIVE THAT MORNING REMINDED ME OF the comforting fact that the worst thing doesn't *always* happen. Standing shakily, it was clear he was not a healthy pig. He was very skinny. His tail didn't curl, but drooped like a dried-up umbilical cord. But he was stronger. He didn't even seem lonely. Normally, wild pigs are gregarious creatures, living in groups called sounders of about twenty animals (though sometimes more than a hundred). Much like elephants, two or more pig families, composed of mothers and their children, may travel, play, feed, and rest together, the sounders staying stable until the mating season (when previously solitary males fight for females, mate, and then, mercifully, leave). On farms, pigs also enjoy the company of their fellows. Pig communities are called drifts—a word I always loved, for it evokes a group of animals moving as one, drifting like a cloud of pigdom over the landscape. Pigs snuggle together when they sleep, and if baby pigs are anxious, they'll stick together so tightly that commercial hog farmers call the phenomenon "squealing superglue."

But for Christopher, it must have been a luxury to spend the night alone. With a spacious, clean, dry pen all to himself, he was unencumbered by the squeal and sprawl of pushy, bigger siblings who always ate all the food. And he probably didn't miss his mother, either—after all, if he complained, there was always the danger she'd bite him in half. It was probably a relief to have escaped from his pig family.

That very first morning, Christopher Hogwood seemed to understand that things had changed for the better. His new family must have looked odd to him—vertical, hairless, and eight nipples short of the proper quota, among other inadequacies. This would require some accommodation, but he seemed game. Calm but curious, he looked at me with his humanlike brown eyes as if to say, "OK—*now* what?"

I was wondering the same thing. But now it seemed a far more hopeful question.

I WAS BURSTING TO TELL MY FATHER ABOUT CHRISTOPHER. My mother had stoically put up with all the creatures I'd had as a child—scaly, biting lizards who would escape while my father was at work and I was at school, parakeets who would perch on the chandelier and splatter droppings on the mahogany dining room table, turtles she'd find swimming with me in my bathwater—but my father truly loved animals. News of our little pig might have taken his mind off his illness.

But I kept Christopher Hogwood a secret. There was no

reason I could think of that my father wouldn't like the pig. But if he hadn't approved of this creature I so tenderly adored, it would have broken my heart—as had happened with my marriage.

I had loved Howard all through college, though I didn't realize it. We had worked together on Syracuse University's daily newspaper, the *Daily Orange*. When Howard was managing editor, he had hired me as an assistant, and later we worked side by side editing the op-ed and editorial pages for eight hours a day, five days a week, for two years. I enjoyed everything about him—his brilliant wit, his bewildering abundance of ideas, his forceful, surprising writing, his commitment to bettering the world. I loved his loud laugh and his bushy black eyebrows and his mass of unruly curls that reminded me of a Cotswold sheep. But we were friends. We'd never dated.

Three months after graduation, with a contract to publish his first book, Howard was temporarily without an apartment. Since I had a job on a New Jersey newspaper and a rented cabin at the edge of a wood, I invited him to stay with me. He said he would only need to stay till Christmas.

He didn't say which Christmas. But in the meantime, each morning he would wake me by playing my favorite record, *Songs of the Humpback Whale,* and place a ferret or two in my bed. By day, we would both write—he at the cabin, me at the newspaper—and phone each other with writing questions. Would this lead work? How to handle that transition? We would both write about fourteen hours a day, often six days a week. We were on fire with words we hoped would elucidate and preserve what we found beautiful and important in the world—its historic and natural landmarks, its wild lands and creatures, our understanding of our place on the planet. Howard inspired me with his dedication and intellect, and delighted me with his gentleness and humor; he came to love my intensity and joy.

Eight years later—after I'd quit the paper, lived for six months in a tent in the Australian outback, rejoined Howard in a rented carriage house at the New Hampshire–Massachusetts border, and moved, again, to the house our friends owned—we were still living together. I had not mentioned this to my parents. I hadn't, in fact, mentioned Howard at all. My mother had strong views about the "right kind" and "wrong kind" of people to "cultivate." This tall, skinny Jewish liberal with wild, curly hair was not one of them.

When we announced our plans to marry, Howard came to Virginia. My father was pained. He knew what was in store. My mother was livid. Speaking to me even more slowly than her Arkansas accent normally flowed, as if belaboring the obvious, she detailed Howard's unsuitability: he didn't have a "real" job, he laughed too loudly, his hair was wild, and his sneakers were coming untied. Then, attempting to sound sympathetic, she added, "And he can't *help* it that he's Jewish."

Howard's parents, on the other hand, had known about me all along. Relieved we were going to legitimize our relationship, they forgave the cross around my neck. They assured me my parents would come around. After all, they said, we were family.

Frankly, family meant little to me. Almost everyone in my extended family was dead before I was born—my father's mother and brother, my mother's father—and those few who survived to my birth lived too far away to often see. If family was really some cohesive, committed unit, how could my parents so adamantly reject the chosen spouse of their only child? To me, family meant a mother and a father and the offspring that biology dealt them—often to their mutual sorrow. I wanted none of it.

After our wedding, which they did not attend, my parents sent me a letter in which they formally disowned me. I can't remember the words—Howard took the letter away—but I remember the shock of seeing the handwriting: it was written in the forceful, familiar, beloved hand of my father.

Why had my father written it? The question plagued me. My father was less prejudiced than most men of his era. He got along with everyone—black, white, Christian, Jew, Yankee, Southerner. He did not even hate the former enemy, the Japanese. But on the issue of my husband, I finally decided, he had capitulated to my mother's vehemence; after all, he lived with her, not me.

We had no communication for two years. And then I got a letter from my father's sister in California. The doctors had found a spot on his lung. I called the hospital, discovered it was cancer, booked the next flight to D.C., and walked into his room at Walter Reed.

My parents were glad to see me. But over the months I would fly back and forth to Virginia to care for my father, both of my parents periodically shot me stinging barbs about my husband.

I wasn't about to give them the chance to insult my pig, too.

EVERYONE ELSE, THOUGH, WAS THRILLED ABOUT CHRISTOPHER. Our friends came over to see him, much the way people come to see a new human baby. But unlike human babies—most of whom, bald, pink, and larval, look exactly like, well, typical human babies—Christopher Hogwood did not look like a typical baby pig. The pastor, Graham Ward, dropped by with his wife, Maggie, and admired Christopher's lavishly furry ears. Eleanor Briggs, a photographer and philanthropist who had founded a conservation center in our town, naming it after Harris, her cat, was impressed with his huge, almost unwieldy head.

But Elizabeth Thomas, a well-known author who had become a friend and mentor in the three years I had known her, was struck most by Christopher's frailty. Liz knew a great deal about animals around the world. She had lived in Africa among the Bushmen of Namibia, studied elephants in South Africa and wolves on Baffin Island. Normally, she knew, baby pigs, like baby warthogs, are as sturdy as little tanks. Christopher was spindly and wobbly, his hips so slender that his back hooves nearly touched. Liz was worried whether Christopher would make it—but, seeing my joy in the piglet, she kept this concern to herself.

Luckily, I had friends whose idea of a good time was to hang out in a pigpen. We'd kneel in the shavings and let him explore our hands with his wet, quivering nose disk. We'd feed him tidbits of apple and carrot and grain. We'd delight in the flexibility of his lips, the lapping of his quick, pink tongue. Even when he would sleep, twitching now and then with piglet dreams, we would stare at him like he was the Yule log on TV, a focal point of communal comfort and joy.

When it got warmer, we'd take him out in the greening grass and watch him mince around on his tiny, perfect hooves. Christopher was silent at first, but after a while, he found his voice and began to emit thrilling little grunts. He'd visibly compress his emaciated belly with each one, like an animated squeaky toy. He began to greet Howard and me in this way, and soon he grunted at the sound of our footsteps approaching his pen. Each morning, when I came to bring his breakfast of warm mash and table scraps, we called to each other:

Chris (*sleepily*): "Unh. Unh. Unh."

Sy: "Good morning, Pig-Boy!"

Chris (*inquiringly*): "Unh-unh-unh? Unh-unh-unh-unh?"

Sy (*closer*): "Your delicious breakfast is coming!"

Chris (*with building excitement*): "Unh! Unh! Unh! Unh!"

Although he was eating well now, Christopher Hogwood stayed remarkably small. When he had arrived, he was about the size of a young, short, skinny cat. After a month with us, he was still cat-sized, though stockier. Maybe, just like Mary said, he would never get terribly large. Which was a good thing, because once the house we were living in was sold, we might have no place to put a great big pig.

REAL ESTATE AGENTS WERE SHOWING US AN INCREASINGLY dis-couraging crop of houses for sale. We had clearly told them what we wanted: an old house, a barn, a little bit of land, a quiet neighborhood—preferably in the town where we were already living.

The village of Hancock embodied all the reasons we had moved to New Hampshire from strip-malled, suburban-ized New Jersey. Much of Howard's writing examined the forces disassembling American places—how we are "using the world's greatest wealth," as he put it, "to create ugliness." We longed for woods and wetlands, fields and farms, and for neighbors who knew each other as well as the land and its history.

A friend had told us that in New Hampshire in the 1980s, you could rent a huge farmhouse for $100 a month. This turned out to be false. Instead, we'd found a little carriage house for $400 a month—an accessory to a huge 1880s Victorian that sat like a beached steamship on a hill on the border of New Hampshire and Massachusetts. The town was then on the cusp of a building boom. Still, we lived there happily for three years until one day disaster struck: our ferrets were stolen from their hutch in the side yard. We tried everything to find them, including hiring a private investigator with our meager funds, to no avail. But the PI told us he'd discovered that people's dogs were also disappearing from the neighborhood, probably being sold to medical research labs. That's when we moved in with two friends, renting half of their two-family farmhouse in Hancock.

Immediately we felt safe. With a two-hundred-year-old, white-steepled meetinghouse, only two stores (a video rental shop and a grocery, the Hancock Cash Market), one full-time cop, and a population of fifteen hundred, this was the sort of place where the only reason you'd lock your car was if you didn't want people leaving zucchini in the backseat while you were at church.

It would be a good place, we now thought, to raise a pig.

But what could we afford? Nothing in town, apparently. And the pickings were slim in surrounding towns. There was Trak-Vu, a dark, low-ceilinged house overlooking abandoned railroad tracks, in whose upstairs bedrooms Howard could not stand upright. Farther away, there were the hastily built A-frames on quarter-acre lots, houses that people used on ski vacations—exactly the sort of development we hated. And we certainly didn't want to build—that would only contribute to the sprawl we had fled. In another town, one agent showed us a house next door to a working quarry. The heavy machinery would only be running weekdays, from nine to five, the agent informed us cheerfully.

Meanwhile, surveyors had descended on the Hancock house, in preparation for putting it on the market. Oddly, they kept coming back. They measured twice, then three times. Howard thought something was up.

But I was only dimly aware of this, as by that time I was shuttling ever more frequently back to Virginia, where my father's last battle raged. Though he never spoke to me of the war, when I'd been a little girl I used to lie awake at night sometimes, wondering whether I could withstand torture. Now, two decades later, I had my answer: yes, I could. Once, at the hospital, medical technicians removed a tube the size of a garden hose from my father's lung. Two men in fatigues yanked it from his chest with such force that the effort threw them against the wall and sent lung fluid spraying across the room. I held my father's hand. He didn't even squeeze it. Neither of us flinched. Neither of us said a word. Afterward, he smiled at me. It was as if he had said: "We can take it. We can do this. We are that tough, you and me."

But despite courage and stoicism, despite surgery and chemo and radiation, the cancer spread to my father's brain. First he could no longer walk, then he could no longer stand. (He could, however, still phone his broker from his bedside, which he did regularly, making stock trades that made my mother increasingly nervous.) My mother, beside herself with fear and rage and grief, increased her martini intake, and we fought bitterly.

On Father's Day, as he lay on his deathbed, I told my father I had finished my book. I read to him the last lines of the acknowledgments: "And finally, I would like to thank my father, Brigadier General A. J. Montgomery, whose idea it was that I make my first trips to Africa and Australia, and in whose intrepid footsteps I falteringly follow."

He died three days later, fighting for breath, as my mother and I held his hands. He was buried in Section 1 of Arlington National Cemetery, with full military honors.

WHILE I WAS AWAY, TWO MAJOR EVENTS TOOK PLACE BACK home—the significance of which would soon prove profound. One was that Howard wormed the pig.

Christopher Hogwood was now four months old, and while he was much stockier, he was still no bigger than a cat— albeit a cat made out of cast iron. Howard knew what to do. Growing up on Long Island before the housing boom eradicated his neighborhood's last farms, on Saturday mornings, awaiting the cartoons, he used to watch *The Modern Farmer.* The show touted the benefits of building modern, hygienic cowsheds. And it stressed the importance of regularly dosing your pigs with medicine to rid them of intestinal worms. If you don't, you're feeding the worms and not the pig.

Twenty years later, *The Modern Farmer* still exhorted my husband to agricultural excellence. He presented himself to the clerk behind the counter at the local Agway feed store.

"Time to worm the swine herd!" Howard announced.

"How many do you have?" asked the sales clerk.

"One," my husband replied confidently.

"Oh." The clerk seemed disappointed, but nonetheless handed over a packet of swine wormer—molasses-flavored pellets that Christopher devoured greedily. In his frail infancy, the medicine hadn't done him any good. But now he was healthy enough to benefit. Thus began the transformation that would change Chris's figure, and our lives, forever. Or, as Howard likes to say, the rest of the story is lard.

The other event that would change our lives was a discovery: Howard found out why the surveyors kept coming back to the house. They couldn't quite make the property come out to eight acres—land enough to subdivide into two lots, according to local zoning laws. This had been our landlords' plan from the start, and the windfall they expected from such a deal was one reason their parents had so eagerly bankrolled the property. For them, it was less a home than an investment.

But the surveyors' measurements kept coming up short. It turned out that a tiny sliver of the land—about the size of a parking space—was actually owned by a neighbor. Our landlords tried in vain to buy it from her. They could not fathom that she might have wanted to keep that land precisely to prevent another house from being built on the open pasture—a place where she and other longtime residents had enjoyed watching horses and sheep graze for decades. In fact, a neighbor's horses were grazing there now, an arrangement that we, as caretakers, maintained in lieu of mowing.

We were delighted that the field would never be turned into some suburban lawn. But we did not realize quite yet what this discovery meant for us: now the price of the house and land were within our reach. Because the landlords and we were friends, we could skip the considerable expense of a real estate agent. Because it was a two-family house, we could rent out half—generating regular money the banks considered far more secure than our irregular incomes as freelance writers. By summer's end, we would buy the farm.

BY THE TIME I RETURNED FROM MY FATHER'S FUNERAL, THOUGH, summer was just beginning. While I'd been gone, the ferns had uncoiled and the violets had bloomed. Thrush song spiraled downward from the edge of the woods, and ovenbirds were crying their familiar "Teacher! Teacher! Teacher!" Exhausted and shaken and empty, I was numb to beginnings when Howard picked me up at the airport that day. But on the way back home, we stopped at a farm to pick strawberries. Before us stretched row after row of plants, laden with juicy, heart-shaped fruits. They felt warm, like the sun, in our fingers. They tasted like life itself. Their fragrance was intoxicating. The very air was like champagne.

I remembered how my father had fought like a soldier for his last gasp of air. I remembered, too, a speech he had given at the commemoration of a memorial for the POWs captured in the Philippines. All these years later, with starvation, captivity, and dehydration so far behind him, still, he told the audience, he would often purposely let his thirst grow sharp—to better relish the delayed delight of a cool, clean glass of water.

He had loved so much in his life: cooking and serving and eating fine food. Cocktail parties, banquets, parades. Golf and swimming and dancing. Travel and music, movies and books. One by one, cancer and chemo stole my father's strength, dulled his senses. But there was always, still, the prospect of a drink of cool water.

My father was not afraid to die. But even in his diminished state, even as Valhalla, that heroes' paradise, beckoned like a finish line to a race well run, I think my father just wanted one last, delicious taste of the sweet breath of life.

And I remembered that now, the sweet, warm New Hampshire summer was waiting for me: a new beginning, fragrant, abundant, and ripe.

I couldn't wait to get home and give Christopher some strawberries. He surely smelled them before he heard me coming around the bend to the barn. But I imagined that his greeting grunts were just as much a welcome for me, as for his food.

He looked wonderful. As he delicately grasped each strawberry in his flexible lips, emitting grunts of pleasure, I saw that his black and white coat had grown glossy, and his tail (though still not curly) now swished from side to side, wagging like a dog's, when he was happy.

During the two weeks I'd been gone, the wormer had

worked its wonders. Christopher's tummy had begun to fill out. His voice had grown deeper and more authoritative. When we let him out, he began to push his nose into the earth and produce impressive divots in the lawn.

To our delight, the Spotted Thing was growing stronger every day.

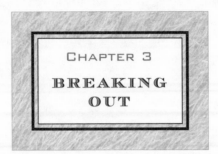

CHAPTER 3

BREAKING OUT

"THERE'S A BLACK-AND-WHITE PIG ROOTING UP OUR LAWN. IS IT yours?"

This is the sort of phone call you don't want to get early on a Sunday morning. But it is also one that cannot be easily ignored.

A pig on the loose—even one not much bigger than a cat—is a force to be reckoned with. Now that Christopher was no longer sick, the power of his little snout was unleashed. It was a force of nature. Christopher would touch a piece of earth with his nose, and an impressive hole would open. With just a step or two, pushing forward with his nose disk, Chris became a miniature bulldozer. The hole became a trench, and the trench became a chasm. Sod peeled away from him as easily as the skin off a banana. And with neighbors' gardens ripening with summer lettuce, beanstalks, broccoli—and by early fall, pigs' favorites, *pumpkins*—the carnage was too awful to contemplate.

"I'll be right there!" I'd promise the caller—and race across the street barefoot and pillow-haired, still in my nightshirt, to scoop Chris up in my arms and carry him back to his pen.

Where he would stay . . . for a while. But not for long.

How Christopher Hogwood staged his escapes was a mystery Howard and I could not initially penetrate. He wasn't bulling through our makeshift gate—he didn't yet weigh enough to do that. What was happening was actually more disturbing. At first, he had learned to untie the string that kept the gate shut. Later we switched to bungee cords, and he had figured out how to undo these (we suspected with his lips, but we never saw). And finally we had installed a bolt that not only slid sideways to close but also required me to flip it downward to fit a curve in the latch into a metal placeholder. Somehow, the little pig had figured out how to push his nose disk and lips between the slats of the gate to open this device *from the inside.*

Truth be told, I was rather proud of his feat. In fact, everything he did thrilled me. In Howard's words, I had gone "hog wild." When I was not actually with Chris or out looking for Chris, I found myself admiring pigs in general. From my extensive personal library on animals, I unearthed stories and pictures of giant forest hogs, hairy, six-hundred-pound pigs of East Africa; red river hogs, long-faced African pigs with elfin ears; babirusas, wild Indonesian pigs whose faces are nearly obscured by a thicket of ivory tusks. (When I raced upstairs to show Howard a babirusa photo, he pronounced it "ugly as sin.")

I finally even told my mother about Christopher. In my

phone calls to Virginia each Sunday after church, I tried to counter her grief with tales of the pig's escapes, what he ate, who came to visit him. He became the star of my weekly letters to her. And in her neat, typewritten replies, my mother always asked after Christopher.

Never did she ask about Howard, though. It was clear my husband wouldn't be welcome in Virginia—and that I wouldn't be going back there anytime soon.

CHRISTOPHER'S MOTIVES FOR ESCAPE WERE AS VEXING AS HIS MYSterious methods. Didn't he like his pen? He had wood shavings and hay into which he could burrow for warmth, and a dirt floor into which he could dig should he prefer to cool off. He always had plenty of fresh water. He always had plenty to eat. When we slid the barn door open each morning, sunlight flooded into the front of the pen during the day, but there was always cool shade at the back. At night he was closed in snugly. What was there not to like?

Maybe he was out looking for us. From his happy greeting grunts and the sparkle in his eyes, we could tell he enjoyed our company. I came out to see him about once every hour or two, to pet him or offer him a treat. I called out to him when I came, but didn't have to. He listened for footsteps. In fact, if we walked anywhere near his pen and did not come over, he would bellow till we did. But Christopher, we thought, did not actually know where we lived. Howard was adamant that the pig should never find out. We never let him see us pass through any of the house's three entrances lest he one day decide to storm through a screen door, seeking our company and discovering the recreational opportunities of upending our refrigerator. We assumed Chris could smell us, though, even when he couldn't see us. Surely he knew we were out there somewhere, and maybe this explained his wanderings.

Or perhaps, we mused, Christopher broke out for the same reason as do many young males. Maybe he was looking for beer.

During the hot summer, we'd often let Chris out with us while Howard was enjoying the occasional cold one. Generously, Howard thought he'd let Christopher try a swig. He figured he'd like it. "After all," Howard reasoned, "what is beer but liquid grain?"

Howard was all too right. Christopher enjoyed his first Rolling Rock, which he slurped out of the bottle. Then he tried a Corona, fitting his lips around the spout like an expert. He liked that, too. He drank a Genesee Cream Ale. Mmmm. Christopher soon discovered that he *loved* beer—to the point that if he saw anyone holding a bottle of any kind, he would chase them until they surrendered and let him suck it dry.

Howard began to make frequent forays to the beer store to buy the cheapest brand he could find. "It's for my pig," my husband would explain to the employees, lest word spread that he had a drinking problem—or, worse, extremely poor taste in beer. The beer guys got to know Howard pretty fast. Each time he would stop in, the clerks would inquire after Christopher's latest weight gain. (This we tracked with a calculation we learned at the swine booth at the county agricultural fair: To get the weight of a pig, you measure the animal's circumference just behind the forelegs, called the heart girth. Then you measure the pig's length, from the base of the ears to the base of the tail. Square the heart girth, then multiply it by the length, and divide the total by four hundred for weight in pounds.) Each time they saw Howard, the beer store employees would calculate how much beer they thought the pig could drink before getting drunk. "Oh my God, he could drink two six-packs!" came the realization after Chris topped 250 pounds. Before long, our pig was an object of some envy. Eventually, they figured with awe that he could do half a keg.

That summer, though, Chris wasn't there yet. But one thing was clear: thanks to the wondrous alchemy of swine wormer combined with Schlitz, by July we could see that Mary's prediction that Christopher would stay small was unlikely.

As Christopher's girth increased, so did our doubts about who was in charge at our house. Not only was Chris destined to vastly outweigh us, but we faced a growing realization that our pig was dangerously, possibly diabolically, brilliant.

THE GENIUS OF PIGS HAS BEEN ADMIRED FOR CENTURIES. PIGS' EX-ceptional intelligence has been noted by no less of an authority on animals than Charles Darwin. "I have observed great sagacity in swine," he wrote, assuring his readers that pigs are at least as smart as dogs. (In fact, in the eleventh through fifteenth centuries, poor people often used pigs in place of hunting dogs, as the latter were permitted only to the English aristocracy. In Jeffrey Moussaieff Masson's wonderful book on the emotional lives of farm animals, *The Pig Who Sang to the Moon,* we learn of a black sow named Slut who lived in the New Forest of Hampshire, England, in the mid-1800s, where she was trained to find, point, and retrieve partridges, pheasant, snipe, and rabbits "as well as the best pointer.")

Some pigs are so smart that people have been known to flock from miles around to witness their wisdom. In the late 1700s, a Scottish shoemaker trained a black pig, touted as the "Pig of Knowledge," to perform amazing acts onstage. The pig, said his manager, could spell, tell time, solve math problems, read flash cards, and even read people's minds—spelling out his findings by pointing to letters with his snout. He probably achieved this feat in the same manner as Clever Hans, a horse who actually couldn't solve math problems as advertised, but who *could* read exceptionally subtle and, in fact, subconscious cues from his beloved owner to give the correct answers. The pig performed in England (often along with a rabbit who beat a drum and a turtle who was trained to fetch), and when he died, his obituary made the *Daily Universal Register,* the daily newspaper of record at the time. The obit claimed this pig had earned more money than any other performer—human or animal—living at the time. In 1797, another Pig of Knowledge appeared on the American stage, and thus began a rage for porcine performers. Pigs toured the country in acrobatic troupes and circuses; they exhibited their brilliance at taverns and wagon stands. They lifted handbells with their mouths to play "Home Sweet Home"; striking wands on the xylophone, they beat out the tunes for "Yankee Doodle Dandy" and "God Save the Queen."

But the porcine intellect shines most brilliantly when applied to pigs' own projects. In her book *Animals in Translation,* autistic savant Temple Grandin, a woman who has applied her considerable talents to the design of humane slaughterhouses, writes of pigs on large farms who are fed one at a time inside small, electronically controlled feeding pens. These pigs wear collars with electronic tags read by a scanner, which in turn opens a gate and then closes it so no other pigs can get in. Once inside the pen, the pig has to put its head close to the trough, where another electronic scanner reads the ID and dispenses the food. A number of pigs have figured out this system, she reports. When they find a loose collar lying on the ground, they pick it up and carry it over to the pen and use it to get inside—just like a person uses an electronic pass at a tollbooth or a token to enter the subway.

But equally astonishing is the behavior of the pigs who *hadn't* figured out the scanning system. These pigs, as the author put it, develop "superstitions" about the feeding trough. They act like baseball players, who are known to perform all sorts of gyrations for good luck before going to bat or throwing a pitch. Some of the pigs "walk over to the feeder and go inside when the door opens, then approach the feed trough and start doing some purposeful behavior like repeatedly stomping their feet on the ground. Obviously," Grandin concludes, "they had food delivered a couple of times when they happened to be stomping their feet, and they'd concluded it was the foot stomping that got them food." To link correlations as cause and effect (even incorrectly, as is the case with much of medicine) is considered a very sophisticated intellectual ability—one that many scientists would prefer to claim animals don't possess.

But those of us who pay attention to animals know better. The New England writer Noel Perrin (best known for his wonderful *First Person Rural* and its sequels) once had a gifted pig whose intelligence found release in art. Perrin had built a low pig house for the animal to provide shade in an outdoor pen, and as a special touch had covered it in shingles. On the first day he presented the structure to the pig, Perrin returned to the pig house in the afternoon to find that the pig had pulled off every one of the shingles. He had carried them some distance away from the house and carefully arranged them on the ground in a pattern that the pig apparently found aesthetically pleasing.

But in Christopher Hogwood's case, it appeared his great talent was not for art but for exploration.

On the phone, at the post office, in the Cash Market, we

would get reports of his travels around town. He'd been to visit the family across the street. He'd gone around the corner by the old railroad trestle and visited the beavers at Moose Brook. He traveled to the state highway to see the folks who owned the Cash Market and lived around the corner. Sometimes people would be out jogging or walking their dogs, find our pig along the road, and bring him back to his pen—and we wouldn't find out until days later.

What was remarkable was not how far he traveled—he never seemed to go more than a quarter mile from our house—but how many people he met, and the indelible impression he always made. Unlike me, Christopher was a naturally gregarious soul who made friends easily. On his jaunts, he became an ambassador of our barnyard. I enjoyed his reflected popularity. Even when he caused trouble, people almost invariably liked him.

One misty morning in early fall, Christopher managed to delay our local representative to the New Hampshire legislature on her way to the statehouse in Concord. Eleanor Amidon, the stately part-time organist for our church, was halfway down her long dirt driveway in her car when a pair of tall, hairy ears hove into view. Looking over the hood of her station wagon, she realized her driveway was blocked by a black-and-white spotted pig.

She was not intimidated—her father had once tried farming pigs in North Leominster, Massachusetts, though he switched back to cattle when he realized how easily pigs escaped. But Eleanor was a lady of a certain age, dressed in her navy blue blazer, blue pumps, and nylons, and about to be late for an appointment. She did what any reasonable, well-dressed professional woman does when confronted with a problem pig: she backed up the car and yelled for her husband.

Dick Amidon, recently retired from his post as chief of

staff for the Speaker of the New Hampshire House of Repre-
sentatives, was as well known in town as his wife. He was
moderator of our annual town meeting, the spring gathering
at which all our registered voters mass at the firehouse to vote
on every cent to be spent that year on town business, and he
was also moderator at our Congregational church. Dick was
now earning a living as a private consultant, working out of
their home—and thus dressed to deal with a pig. As he came
out the door, Chris moved out of the driveway and advanced
toward his goal: the Amidons' lettuce garden.

Of their several gardens, the Amidons' lettuce patch is the
one closest to the house—strategically placed so that Eleanor
and Dick could enjoy their fresh-picked produce within seconds of plucking it from the ground. Christopher Hogwood
apparently had the same idea. When I came up the driveway
looking for him, I found Dick with his arms wrapped around
the pig's head, trying to steer him away from the lettuce. Chris
was grumbling at him loudly.

"You've got to be careful with pigs, you know," Dick told
me later. "They can be pretty fierce. But not Christopher.
There's not a vicious bone in his body."

Many animals, understandably, bite you if you stand between them and food. Christopher wanted that lettuce. I was
very impressed that under these circumstances, Christopher
was not even trying to bite my neighbor.

So was Dick. "You know, I thought about it later, Sy, and
it dawned on me why he and I got along so well," he mused.
Dick and Eleanor used to be quite active in the Republican
party, but Dick later switched his allegiance to the Libertarians. "If there's ever been an example of a Libertarian pig, that's
Christopher," he said. "He's his own person, he doesn't want
overregulation—all the things that Libertarians look for. He's
a free spirit."

That he was. One time Howard looked out the upstairs window from the spare bedroom he uses as his office. "Ah, there goes so-and-so," he thought, noting a passing jogger. "There goes such-and-such in her car. . . . There goes Chris."

Wait! *Chris?*

We both ran outside.

EARLY IN OUR CAREERS AS SWINEHERDS, WE THOUGHT ABOUT building a fence for our pig. But fencing swine is notoriously difficult—a fence must be very strong indeed to keep a pig from pushing it down or excavating beneath it. But again, Gretchen came to our rescue. She had just the thing. She showed up one day with a small section of electric mesh fencing, eighty feet of it, just as a demo. "This," she promised confidently, "will solve all your problems."

Unlike the strand or two of electric wire used to fence horses, electric mesh ensures the pig can't dig under or leap over the fencing, she said. Pigs quickly learn to respect the boundaries from the first electric shock they receive on touching it. Because the fencing is so easy to set up, it's also easy to expand the pigpen and move it around to afford fresh pasture whenever needed.

"Will it hurt him?" I asked dubiously. "I don't want to even try it if it might hurt him."

"No," she assured me as she set up the fence to form a little corral outside the barn. "It won't hurt him at all. He'll touch it with his nose and get a tiny shock, and he'll back off right away."

"Are you sure?"

"He'll figure it out immediately," Gretchen said as she set up the electric charger. "I've never known an animal not to. Don't worry. You'll see. Watch."

She plugged the extension cord into the socket. I opened Christopher's gate and stepped over the three-foot-tall fencing to the other side.

Chris ran right over to greet us, hit the electric fence with his sensitive nose, and shrieked in pain.

He did not stop shrieking. Nor did he back off. He pushed harder and harder at the fence, using his too-big spotted head as a battering ram against the pain. His screams undulated in frequency, in time with the pulse of the current: *"Ree! Ree! Ree! . . . Ree! Ree! Ree!"*

I joined in immediately. *"Stop! Stop! Stop! . . . Pull the Plug!"* For those few seconds—which felt to me like many minutes—Chris and I could have drowned out a jackhammer. The neighbors must have decided that an ax murderer in our yard was butchering us both.

Gretchen unplugged the extension cord. Chris was fine, if a bit dazed, but I was a wreck.

"Oh, dear," said Gretchen, "I guess that's not going to work after all."

Some species simply cannot walk backward—nine-banded armadillos, for example, can *hop* backward but not walk. But this is not the case with pigs. Nor was Chris's reaction due to a failure of intellect. But what had happened gave me an important insight into the emotional life of this strange little barrel-shaped, cloven-hoofed creature who had transformed us from a couple to a family.

Now I understood what it means to be pig headed.

Christopher Hogwood was a creature of his convictions. When he wanted something, he went, well, whole hog. And what he wanted—whether it was us, or beer, or simply freedom—was on the other side of that fence.

. . .

I KNOW THE ALLURE OF THE OTHER SIDE OF THE FENCE. I ONCE spent six months in a state of almost perfect freedom, on the other side of the world, living in a condition that Howard considered "feral."

After I graduated from college and had worked for five years at the *Courier-News,* my father gave me the gift of a ticket to Australia. I decided to join an Earthwatch expedition—becoming a paying layman working with scientists—assisting with a Chicago Zoological Society study of the habitat of the rare southern hairy-nosed wombat in the scrub desert of South Australia. I loved it so much that the principal investigator, biologist Pamela Parker, offered me a chance to conduct my own studies there. She couldn't pay me or cover my airfare, but she would let me eat for free. I quit my newspaper job and moved to a tent in the outback.

When I arrived, I didn't know what I would study. But one day, as I was alone collecting plant samples for another researcher, I looked up and saw three flightless, four-foot-tall, ostrichlike birds curiously approaching me, less than fifteen yards away. Emus. It was love at first sight.

They could have killed me. With their strong legs, emus can run forty miles an hour and sever fencing wire with a single kick. But incredibly—even though they are more closely related to dinosaurs than to people, even though I had nothing to offer them—these giant birds tolerated my company. They let me follow them. I was able to find them day after day, eventually walking beside them at a distance of only a few feet, recording their every move. No one had ever done this before.

Each observation was a revelation: each choice of berry or seed, each posture of their black periscope necks, each time one combed a feather through its beak to preen. I tried to see the outback through the emus' mahogany eyes, their vision forty times more acute than my own. I felt my senses come alive.

Soon I was so hooked I didn't even want to leave the emus long enough to take the weekly trip to shower at the nearest town.

I had gone wild, and I am sure I looked it. So that the birds would recognize me, I made a point of wearing the same clothes every day: my father's Army jacket, the shirt I'd slept in, my blue jeans, a red bandana. There were no mirrors in camp, and I forgot to brush my hair for so long that I developed a giant mat in the back like you'd find in the fur of a stray dog. But as I wandered through the emus' stark desert world with my runny nose and filthy clothes and matted hair, I felt whole, even beautiful, for the first time in my life.

Not that I wasn't sometimes lonely. I was acutely aware that Howard, the ferrets and the lovebirds, my parents, and my friends were halfway around the world. My day was their night, and my winter their summer. We even slept beneath different stars. But, far away from everything I knew, I felt cleansed and open. I was hungry to fill my emptied soul with the dramas of this new place: its parched orange soil, its thorny acacias, and the lives of the alien creatures with whom I had fallen deeply and passionately in love.

When I left the emus, I wept for days. This was the story of my life: I was always leaving. Unlike Howard, who had lived in the same house on Long Island since the day his parents brought him home from Huntington Hospital, I didn't know what it was like to belong to one place. I had not even been born in this country, but in Germany, where my father was stationed at Frankfurt. The longest my family had stayed anywhere was Quarters 225, Fort Hamilton, Brooklyn, New York—a house my parents didn't own—for just over four years. Even after my father retired from the military, we kept moving—New Jersey, Virginia, then back to Jersey again—as he shifted jobs in the shipping business. No wonder all my childhood pets had never been bigger than Molly, the Scottish terrier with whom I grew up like a sister. Everyone had to be portable. Never had I been rooted enough to commit to a really large animal.

I loved travel, I loved exploring, and I loved wildness. But now, in Hancock, with a pig in the barn, I would find the other piece of my heart's lifelong yearning: home.

HOWARD AND I GAVE UP ON THE FENCE FOR CHRISTOPHER. Instead, we fitted him with a harness devised for a small dog—which we later traded for one for a medium dog and then one for a large dog. We hooked him up to a tether at the edge of the woods in back of what was once a chicken shack and now a little studio. We called the area the Pig Plateau. Tied to an ash tree, stretching twenty feet long, the tether afforded Christopher access to both shade and sun, grass and brush. The location even featured a nice mud wallow in a seep from Moose Brook. Here, Christopher could root to his heart's content. The whole area quickly came to resemble Vietnam after the Tet offensive.

Chris seemed to like the tether arrangement. He liked his yard. He also liked wrapping the rope around a tree in such a way as to create the precise combination of pressure and tension that would release the metal clasp from his harness and allow him to run free.

LOOSE PIGS WERE SOMETHING ALL AMERICANS KNEW ABOUT A couple of hundred years ago, and not just in the country. New York's financial district was named for the long, permanent wall erected in 1652 to restrict the travels of lower Manhattan's free-roaming hogs, along which Wall Street was later built. Loose swine were once a part of every American city. Pigs grew fat for the dinner table while cleaning public spaces of garbage. Pretty much everyone liked it until the pigs got bossy and began to crowd people off the sidewalks.

In the early days of our village, "for many years the settlers permitted their swine to run at large," reports *The History of Hancock, New Hampshire, 1764–1889*. "That the swine of those days had unusual privileges granted them, the following incident in the life of Moses Dennis, Sr., will show," writes the author William Willis Hayward. "It was his duty one year to serve the notices of the annual training. In the discharge of it, as he was entering one of the log cabins, which being without windows was somewhat dark, he suddenly found himself most unceremoniously caught up and carried out backwards, and as unceremoniously set down. He was so taken by surprise that at first he could not comprehend the meaning of his strange reception. He soon discovered that a hog in the house had been frightened by his entrance and in his haste to escape, ran between his legs (which were very short ones), caught him up and deposited him as before stated."

By 1786, though, things changed. That year, an important new office was instituted in our village: the post of hog reeve. At that time, just about every settlement of any size had at least one hog reeve—a sort of sheriff whose duty it was to capture and corral troublemaking hogs. Ten years later, Hancock, with a human population of just over six hundred, needed no fewer than six hog reeves to keep local pigs under control.

Alas, by the time Christopher arrived in Hancock, the office of hog reeve had long since been retired. But, happily, we had Ed Coughlan. Ed was our police chief. For eleven years, he was Hancock's only full-time cop.

Ed was well suited to the task. He was a local guy—he had worked as a small-equipment operator for the state highway department, and raised a family in town with his pretty, blue-eyed wife. With his boyish straight brown bangs, soulful blue eyes, and gentle, modest manner, he had none of the "Step aside, I'm in charge here" brusqueness that police academies seemed to train for. True, he'd had to go to the police academy in Concord for twelve weeks once he was promoted to chief— but most of the job, he said, was "just plain common sense. I have plenty of that," he told me one day. "I just don't have any other kind."

Happily, Hancock offers a cop little chance to battle hard-core crime. Policing the village poses different challenges. For one thing, a number of our elderly residents are losing their eyesight, and as a result frequently hit buildings, cars, and sometimes people while driving their cars. One of our venerable citizens, a former piano teacher who was over ninety years old and legally blind, hit and injured a flagman working on the road. Sometimes they hit each other. One sweet elderly lady, attempting to park at the post office, instead drove past the loading dock, over an embankment, and thumped down on the entrance to the town "beach" on Norway Pond. When Ed came to the scene, he noticed some orange paint on her car. "Where did that come from?" he asked. "Oh, that was where I hit someone last week," she replied calmly.

Ed couldn't be everywhere, but at least one other resident did her best to help police the streets. A short, sometimes grumpy, heavyset woman in her thirties with big blue eyes, she liked to stand in the middle of Main Street in front of the Cash Market and direct traffic. Out-of-towners always obeyed her, not realizing that they were trusting the direction and speed of their car to a person who was mentally retarded. Then there was the sweet, stocky, gray-haired heiress who walked around town in all seasons wearing a tentlike housedress, short socks, and sturdy, well-worn boots. Everyone knew she wasn't quite right, but she had a kind heart. She was often seen at the post office mailing candy to cheer the families of missing children listed on milk cartons, or at the store buying thirty rolls of toilet paper that a clerk would then have to carry to her house.

Ed kept an eye out for these folks, and for everyone else, too. He was like a favorite uncle called in to mediate family squabbles. Even big-city cops will tell you that domestic disturbances are among the most dangerous situations an officer can face, and Ed handled plenty of these. But no problem was too big or too small, as you could see in the local paper, which prints the police log. Some typical excerpts: A squirrel in a garage on Main Street. (It was gone by the time Ed got there.) A turtle on the yellow line on the state highway. (Its removal at 3 p.m. was duly noted.) A child was heard screaming from inside a house. (He didn't want to eat his dinner.) Things are pretty much the same in surrounding towns. In Peterborough, the police log recently reported someone had called 911 because a guinea pig was locked in a car at the hospital parking lot on a hot day. The window was down, but the guinea pig had no water. (People suspected I was the caller, but I wasn't.)

In our town, animals seem to require regular policing—from stray dogs to treed cats, and one summer an injured bobcat. Officer Steve Baldwin took that call. A bobcat had been hit by a car on Route 123. He scooped up the unconscious animal, wrapped her in a blanket, and laid her on the front seat of the cruiser as he sped to the vet. "Then she suddenly woke up," Steve said, "and I knew I had made a mistake." Luckily, the bobcat was in no mood to fight. Steve was able to get her broken hip repaired by veterinary specialists. He was present six months later at her release back into the wild, at the same spot he had rescued her.

Ed had led llamas, ponies, and cattle back home so often that he started to keep a bucket of grain in the trunk of the cruiser. But ours was the first loose pig of his police career.

On a warm September afternoon, Ed got a call about a pig in the road. The caller was pretty sure whose pig it was. Ed found Chris out by Route 137 down by Mike Cass's driveway. He parked the cruiser and tied a rope to the pig's neck, planning to lead him home.

Christopher, however, had other plans. "He didn't want to go at first," Ed said. This was a problem, because by that time Christopher weighed more than Ed did. "He wasn't aggressive," Ed said, "but he was pretty determined."

When it became evident that Christopher was not easily taken into custody, Ed, calling on his abundant common sense, decided to wait. After a few minutes, Christopher changed his mind. In fact, his change of mind was emphatic. Chris took off at a brisk trot, pulling Ed on the rope behind him like a boat pulls a water skier.

Impressed by the sight of a uniformed police officer running along the road behind a young spotted pig, a driver stopped his car on the road and called out.

"What are you going to do with the pig?" he asked Ed.

"He's going to do whatever he wants," Ed replied, still running. "I'll just follow him!"

Happily, Christopher was more of a sprinter than a marathoner. When the pig slowed down, Ed had a chance to notice some green apples beneath the tree on the triangle of ground between our street and Route 137. He pocketed a few of these and fed them to Christopher.

By the time we saw Ed and Chris coming up our road (we had been out looking for him in the opposite direction), they were walking together like old friends.

After that, Ed always kept some apples in his cruiser, too.

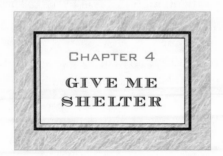

CHAPTER 4

GIVE ME SHELTER

EVEN BEFORE CHRISTOPHER'S FIRST SUMMER WITH US ENDED, WE realized our lives had become decidedly pig-centric.

We spent a lot of time with Chris. Mornings, before making our breakfast, I'd feed him first thing. It was a great way to start our day. He was always delighted with whatever I gave him—pig and sow pellets, stale muffins, banana peels. I was always delighted to watch him eat. For a few minutes, I would listen to the music of his lips slapping against his food before I returned to the kitchen for our own breakfast. Afterward, if the day was sunny, I would carry (and later lead) him down to the Pig Plateau. While Howard and I wrote, Chris would root, graze, sleep, wallow—and await our return. Or, perhaps, plot an escape.

How often we interacted with Chris during our writing day depended on a number of factors—most of them, like our pig, beyond our control. If he broke out, visiting with his growing circle of friends, we might spend an hour or more looking for him. This was enormously disruptive, of course, but our relief when he came home to us—and our gratitude to anyone who helped return him—erased any trace of anger over the lost time.

But even if he did not escape, our hours were increasingly ruled by our pig's needs. If he did not like the weather—he hated to be rained on—he would call for us to let him back in his pen. We would drop everything, midsentence, to rescue him.

We checked on him roughly once an hour. Was he getting too much sun? Pigs' skin can sunburn like a person's. Had he wrapped his tether around a tree? We'd have to untangle him. Did he need a drink of water? Did he need petting? Sometimes these checks led to pig petting sessions that might last fifteen minutes or more, whether Chris needed it or not. (I always did.) Soon our feet wore a path in the grass from the back door to the barn, and another from the barn to the Pig Plateau.

Of course, having a new member in your family always changes your life. They need feeding and cleaning and time and love. But because our new arrival was a pig, the change was particularly profound—because his needs were expanding as fast as his weight. And so was the growing circle of friends and family that would help us.

BY THE FIRST AUTUMN OF HIS LIFE, CHRISTOPHER'S EXPONENTIAL growth had made it obvious that he would soon not only be able to escape, but also to completely destroy his makeshift pen in the barn. Earlier that summer, we had seen him walk through the wooden lattice beneath our front porch like Casper the Friendly Ghost. (That's where we and our twenty-something tenants, Mary Pat and John Szep, stored our garbage before we took it to the dump on Sundays, and one day Chris had smelled something especially appealing: to our mortification, it was the odiferous wrapper from our tenants' last package of breakfast bacon.)

Howard knew what had to be done, but the scale of the project, and my well-documented ineptitude with power tools, made this a job that demanded an expert.

So we summoned a retired engineer from America's top avionics corporation. Howard's dad, a veteran of Sperry Rand Corporation, drove up from Long Island. He made a point not to mention the purpose of his northward journey to his rabbi: he was going to help his son build a palace for a pig.

I'd been a little worried about how Howard's parents might feel about Christopher. After all, they were observant Jews, sufficiently Orthodox to keep separate plates and silverware for milk and meat in their home. It was enough that they had to tolerate a shiksa wife—but a pet pig?

To my relief, they had no problem with Chris. "Just don't eat him," said my father-in-law. When it came to pigs, at least, I was in perfect accordance with the code of Leviticus.

Before his parents got here for Operation Pig Palace, Howard and I shifted things all over the barn, looking for hardware and lumber we might use. Useful items abounded, but they were not always easy to extract. One day, in an attempt to rescue a four-outlet box, we untangled a huge ball consisting of a tiller wrapped in a black wire spliced into a yellow wire, which ran into an orange wire, which was attached to the outlet box—all of it entwined with an old ball of rope. Beneath us, Chris bellowed all the while, as if we had forgotten him entirely.

In fact, Christopher bellowed for much of the next four days.

Sensibly, Howard and his dad were building the new pen on the site of the old one—which of course meant the pig had to be temporarily evicted. Normally he would have been happy out on his Pig Plateau. But, although Chris couldn't actually see the work crew in his pen, he knew something was going on. A pig's sense of smell is so refined that piglets know not only the scent of their mothers, but the scent of the particular teat that becomes their own personal feeding station. Experimenters have found that pigs who have nuzzled plastic cards can pick them out from a deck days later, even after the cards have been washed. Pigs' hearing, too, is excellent—with a frequency range that extends far above those of humans, and probably significantly below as well—and Chris's huge, rotating ears acted like radar dishes, tracking and pinpointing sounds. So it must have been obvious to him that a travesty was under way: something interesting was happening inside *his* pen—and he wasn't there to supervise.

To Howard and me, the meaning of Christopher's bellows were completely clear: "Hey. Hey! *Hey!* That's *my* pen! What's going on? Hey-y-y-y-y!"

WORKING NINE-HOUR DAYS, HOWARD AND HIS DAD ERECTED A PEN worthy of *Sty Beautiful.* Inside the barn, they framed out walls with oversized lumber. With pink fiberglass we found in the barn's upper loft, they insulated the walls to an R-value of 22 (our house, in contrast, was insulated only to R-12). Modifying the setup Gretchen had originally erected from pallets, they installed a front gate on strong hinges. They put in a light.

My mother-in-law and I mostly hid inside the house, ostensibly cooking, for fear the men would ask us to hold some heavy, splintery object exactly two inches off the ground and keep it *perfectly still* while they hit it with a hammer. But we knew the building project was well supervised. While the pig bellowed at them from afar, the men were being scrutinized at close range by sixteen orange eyes, belonging to the eight shiny black hens we called the Ladies.

Gretchen had given them to us as a housewarming present. The Ladies looked like a small flock of cheerful nuns—if nuns had crimson combs and orange eyes and scaly yellow feet. With industry and precision, the Ladies pecked at bugs and seeds around the barnyard, stole scraps from Christopher's bowl when he wasn't looking, and generally kept the pig company when Howard and I were in the house writing. By fall, the hens were giving us eighty delicious brown eggs every week. But what we loved most about them was the way they greeted us.

"Do they *know* you?" Howard's dad had asked in astonishment the first time he saw the Ladies in action. "I didn't think chickens were that smart!" Howard's dad and mom had both grown up in the Bronx, where local experience with chickens was largely confined to the soup pot. But he was soon to expand his knowledge. Because Gretchen had raised these hens from chicks, and Howard and I had visited them almost daily during their upbringing, they didn't just *know* us; they were our biggest fans. When the Ladies saw us coming, they would race toward us, their wings held slightly open, and mob us as if we were the Beatles. Howard's dad really got a kick out of it. The Ladies believed we were bringing them cottage cheese, which was often true. Once they had finished all the cheese, wearing the avian equivalent of a milk moustache, they would wipe their amber beaks on the ground—or, endearingly, on my pants—and return to bug hunting, narrating their explorations all the while in their lilting chicken language.

During most days, the Ladies were free to wander the property, whose boundaries they instantly intuited (and, unlike Christopher, respected). They did not cross the street. They did not hop over the stone wall to the yard next door—even though that house was vacant. But during Operation Pig Palace, they restricted their travels largely to the area directly beneath Howard and his dad's feet. The Ladies were fascinated by the shiny nails and liked to peck at them, and they seemed transfixed by the men's tools, perhaps imagining the point of the project was to unearth more and larger worms than they were scratching up with only their feet. And not only were the chickens clearly observing the building project; they also seemed to be discussing it, querying and clucking with approval. Their interest was so appealing that Howard's dad—previously not the sort of person you'd expect to find talking to a chicken—began to address them directly. "Excuse me," he would say in a gentlemanly, respectful voice as he bent his six-foot frame to lift a board on which a chicken was standing. "Pardon me," he would murmur before he put his foot down where a couple of hens pecked and puttered. Soon he found himself helping Howard to erect a Chicken Chalet for them in addition to the Pig Palace.

By the time Howard's parents left, the Pig Palace was complete, and the Chicken Chalet nearly so. "It was a unique experience," Howard's dad said of the building project, with a big smile. Admittedly, the pay wasn't great—scrambled eggs, vegetarian lasagna, and apple pie—but at least the hens were more consistently cheerful and encouraging than had been his supervisors at Sperry. Working on government contracts, he said, he had certainly toiled on pork-barrel projects before—but this was his first for an actual pig.

. . .

"Is your pig smart?" people would ask us.

"He's smarter than we are," Howard and I would readily admit. "He's figured out how to get a staff of two college-educated people working for him full time and for free."

Even away from home, our servitude continued. We were always working the slops circuit.

Sure, we kept a sack of pig and sow pellets around, and Chris liked this fine. But pigs, like people, relish variety. And like our thrifty Yankee neighbors, we welcomed the idea of feeding our pig good food that otherwise would be thrown away. Unlike George and Mary, we didn't have enough pigs to consume truckloads of expired Twinkies from a manufacturer, or an entire elementary school's worth of discarded macaroni and cheese. But there were other places to score slops, and these we ambitiously mined.

One site was the post office. Our silver-haired, blue-eyed postmistress, Pat Soucy, was an avid gardener and talented cook. When she had accumulated enough watermelon and cantaloupe rinds, broccoli stalks, and potato peelings, she'd bring them to work in a bucket, and Howard would pick it up when he drove the mile into town for the day's mail. Sometimes, on fine, warm days, Pat would come along with the slops on her lunch break. She'd eat with us at our picnic table under the big silver maple, while Chris ate his lunch on the Pig Plateau.

Then there were parties. I used to dread them. I could never think of anything appropriate to say. My innate idea of a great conversation starter is something like "A blue whale's tongue weighs as much as an elephant!" This opener often causes strangers to move away. Another party strategy that I've found doesn't work is staring at the floor. At one reception I had to attend because I was getting an award, I stared at the floor so intently that other people thought I had dropped something and offered to help me look for it.

But now—thanks to Chris—I had a mission at parties. Finally, I had something to talk about.

I didn't even have to bring it up. Often, when we met new people, our hostess would introduce us: "And this is Sy and Howard. They have a pig." The questions would naturally follow:

"What kind of pig is he?" (There are more than three hundred different pig breeds from around the world, from the fat Poland China developed in Ohio to the long-bodied Yorkshire from England. From New Zealand breeders come the small, docile Kune-Kunes, with cute dewlaps hanging from the lower jaw. From the Austro-Hungarian Empire came the fleecy-coated Swallow-Bellied Mangalitsa, bred for meat suited to Hungarian salami. But as for Chris, Howard would answer confidently, "Hampshire Hill hog," which is not actually a breed, but was Howard's shorthand for describing George's pigs, swine of mixed parentage, bred for sweetness of spirit.)

"How much does he weigh?" (We would give the latest tally.)

"Does he live in the house?" ("No, but if you saw the inside of the house you might think so.")

And always, the question we waited for: "What does he eat?" ("As much as he possibly can.")

Here we began our subtle pitch. We explained what Christopher liked and didn't like. For some reason, he eschewed all members of the onion family, including scallions, leeks, and shallots. He wouldn't eat citrus fruit. And we didn't let him eat meat.

Pigs don't need meat. Although in the wild, pigs will happily devour any carcass or any tasty, helpless animal they come across, they don't usually hunt on their own. Their teeth—blade-shaped incisors and grinding molars, like ours—show that pigs, like us, are true omnivores and can live long, healthy lives fueled by vegetables, fruits, grain, nuts, beans, and roots, just like we can. Because I don't buy meat, Howard and I never had meat leftovers, of course. But I also asked folks who donated garbage to weed out the meat.

Why? The answer was simple: pig manure. (This might not seem like a good topic of conversation for a dinner party, but we live in New Hampshire.) Meat, I would explain to my fascinated audience, makes pig manure smell bad. A vegetarian pig's manure has a nice earthy smell to it, as well as a pleasant shape and texture, rather like a small loaf of braided bread. But add meat to the diet, and it stinks, gets all sticky, and falls through the tines of the pitchfork. It also ruins the compost pile. Do you add dog droppings to the tomato patch in the summer? Of course not. But a vegetarian pig's manure is garden gold.

At this point in the party conversation, invariably someone would ask, "Well, what are you going to do with him?"

I generally bristled at the question. "What are you going to do with your grandson?" I wanted to fire back. "Looks to me he might dress out at maybe fifty or sixty pounds."

But Howard kept me in check. "We're going to send him to the Sorbonne," he would reply. And then we would explain that since I was a vegetarian and Howard was a Jew, with Christopher we would explore the largely uncharted territory of just how long a pig can naturally live. Possibly because Chris had no reason to be suspicious about our motives, we explained, he was an exceptionally gracious, well-adjusted, and cheerful pig.

"Oh, you would love him!" we would promise. "Come see him anytime! And don't forget to bring your garbage." We promised "dinner and a show." They brought Christopher's dinner. Watching him eat it was the show.

If he was in his pen when people arrived, the opening act was Christopher's enthusiastic exit. "Look, Pig Man, you've got visitors!" I would tell him, and Chris would answer with excited grunts. My announcement was unnecessary; he could clearly hear and smell the people coming, as well as their slops, and he could hardly wait. When I opened his gate, he shot out like a squealing black and white cannonball. I would race him with the slops bucket to the Pig Plateau. Here I would pour out some slops, giving me time to hook the tether to his harness. Then we could all stand back—a step or two beyond the reach of his tether—and enjoy the spectacle.

When it came to eating, Christopher was a performance artist.

Watching a pig eat is the ultimate vicarious thrill. Seldom can you take such pleasure in another's joy. Here is someone following his bliss. Pigs are quite literally made for eating—they were bred to eat and get fat fast. (Of all mammals, domestic pigs are the most efficient at converting plant food into flesh: a piglet can gain five pounds a day—a pound for every three pounds of plant food he eats; a calf needs to eat ten pounds for a similar gain.) Grunting, slurping, and snorting with delight, Christopher ate with the enthusiasm of a gourmand and the natural grace of an athlete. Food wasn't just the number one thing on his list; we figured food occupied numbers one through perhaps fifty on his hierarchy of desires.

We humans aren't allowed to enjoy food this much. To do so is labeled the sin of gluttony, and its consequence, if we are to believe the magazines, is clogged arteries, shapeless couture, and guilt. For many of us, food is the enemy. But while Christopher was eating, it seemed he was communing with his Higher Power. It was a beautiful thing to see.

No wonder our visitors often wanted to hand-feed Christopher. It was their way of joining in the fun. Long objects were safest: loaves of stale French bread, overripe bananas, overgrown zucchini—Chris didn't bite, but it was wise to put distance between his eager mouth and your hand. (Small round foods, like cupcakes and apples, were best hand-fed when he was in the pen, when he would hold his mouth open so you could toss food in like a basketball.) These Chris would bite forcefully, but his next response depended on whether or not you let go of the other end. He liked you to hold on to the French bread, so he could tear away a bite-sized piece, using your grip the way human diners employ knife and fork. With denser, harder items such as zucchini and large carrots, he simply bit into them and expected you to keep the other half from falling on the ground. Not that he had an aesthetic problem with eating food off the dirt; he just liked the extra interaction when you fed him the next piece and, if it was big enough, the piece after that.

Most of his meals, however, were too gooey or amorphous for hand-feeding; these we plopped into his bowl in the pen or poured onto the ground. The uninitiated might think that pigs just Hoover everything up. That was not the case with Hogwood. Unless the foods had commingled in the slops bucket to the point that they were indistinguishable, he carefully chose the items he liked best first, lifting them rather delicately, albeit noisily, with his flexible lips: pasta, pastry, cheese, and fruit. (From an early age, he had a sweet tusk.) Next best were carrots and starches, including rice and potatoes—especially if they had acquired, either in their original preparation or during their stay in the slops bucket, some kind of creamy sauce. Lastly, though still with flourish, he would eat the leftover kale, broccoli, spinach, and the like. If there was any trace of onion or a scrap of lemon or orange peel, he would leave this untouched. If the meal contained any unpeeled eggs, he would crunch them up and then slowly and delicately spit out the shells.

When presented with an item so large or tough he could not immediately bite it in half—a pumpkin, for instance—Christopher would pick it up and shake it, exactly as a dog shakes a sock (and for the same reason: it's a kill gesture, to break the neck of the imaginary prey). The shake-and-kill response was especially effusive when Christopher was presented with an unlikely meal of lobster—more precisely, lobster-flavored exoskeleton. One day, friends came with several guests and their big black dog to see what Chris would do with the remains of the previous night's feast. Christopher picked up an enormous carapace as if he had been dining on lobster all his life. He shook it forcefully from side to side, sending forth a spray of melted butter and causing the lobster's antennae and eye stalks to roust about in a gruesome, lifelike manner. Like a seal with a fish, he gave the lobster a brief toss before catching it again in his mouth, and then pulverized the red exoskeleton with his powerful jaws. Everyone was enthralled, but especially our friend the food writer. Even when he later became a professional chef, seldom did he get to see anyone enjoy a meal as much as Christopher did.

And when presented with foods of even larger dimensions? Imagine our excitement when the family of a seventh-grade gorilla enthusiast, whom I had met on my first book tour, drove out from their home in Saugus, Massachusetts, to visit us. As a present, they brought a fruit basket full of melon balls, beautifully carved from the shell of an enormous watermelon, which must have weighed twenty-five pounds. As it happened, my friend Liz Thomas's sixtieth birthday was the next day—and the day after that we would celebrate the birthday of her anthropologist mother, Lorna, who would be ninety-three. This presented a quandary, as it did every year. Liz was a bestselling author (*The Harmless People* on the Bushmen and *Warrior Herdsmen* on the Dodoth were still in print after three decades, and her newest books, a set of Paleolithic novels, were instant hits); she could afford anything she wanted. Surely Lorna, after ninety-three years, had acquired everything she wanted, too. I'd had no idea what to get for them, but now I had the perfect gift: I would invite them over to watch Christopher eat the remains of the watermelon.

He did not disappoint us. Chris was already in position when Liz and Lorna drove up. Liz helped Lorna walk with her cane out to the Pig Plateau. I carried the huge melon from the refrigerator and placed the hollowed-out giant before him. Christopher bit into it joyfully. With a grunt, he picked it up. He shook it. Pieces of the watermelon flew in all directions, as dramatic as fireworks. With each new bite, sweet juice mixed with his foamy drool and flowed down his jowls like pink champagne on New Year's Eve. And, of course, the action was accompanied by the festive chewing, grunting, slurping, and snorting of a happy pig.

It was a huge hit.

Liz and Lorna both loved animals. Liz had studied animals all over the world, and she and her husband, Steve, had shared their home over the years with a kinkajou (a South American relative of the raccoon, with a grasping tail), a dingo, a team of huskies, two large iguanas, six orphaned possums, and at present two dogs and four cats. (Lorna was more than welcome there, too, but still insisted on living at her own house across from Harvard University—the better to finish her scholarly analysis of her family's pioneering studies of the Bushmen. When Lorna wanted to visit New Hampshire, she drove the two and a half hours up to Liz and Steve's house.)

Lorna loved animals and they loved her, too: whenever Lorna came over to our house, our cockatiel would fly immediately to Lorna's snowy white hair and ride around on her like an animated beret.

Liz had been one of Christopher's special friends ever since he first came to live with us. Like Gretchen, Liz was an indispensable consultant on matters porcine. It was Liz who had taught me how to induce Christopher to lie down. It didn't work under all conditions—if Chris was in the middle of eating, for instance, no earthly force could stop him. But generally, Liz showed me, if you rub a pig along his inguinal region—the area of the belly just in front of the back legs, particularly along the nipples—he will almost irresistibly drop to his front knees, and then, with a thud, fall over onto his side, succumbing to a swoon of pleasure. This intimate caress is almost hypnotic for species across the mammalian spectrum, Liz told me—probably because it emulates the feeling of the mother licking her baby clean, which is often done after nursing. (I later discovered it's effective even on rhinos, experimenting on a captive animal I met while visiting a sanctuary in Texas.)

Of course, Christopher wanted you to keep rubbing his belly forever. In fact, doing so was tempting for everyone. Who would not wish to continue such an exchange of comfort and joy? Never could you find anyone more responsive to caresses. His bliss was contagious.

"Good, good pig," we would croon to our prone beast as we rubbed him, loving as a lullaby. "Good, good pig. Good big pig. Fine, fine swine. Good, good, gooood." He would grunt back to us in exactly the same rhythm, slowing down as he lolled toward slumber.

Belly rubs were usually the grand finale to all of Christopher's public eating performances. And, of course, this is what we did after Christopher finished Liz and Lorna's birthday watermelon.

But first, Howard took a photo to commemorate the event. We lined up to face the camera in ascending seniority: Christopher, age one; me, thirty-three; Liz, sixty; Lorna, ninety-three. "We're all thirty years apart," Liz observed. "Yes, here we are," said Lorna, "four generations." It felt for all the world like a family photo. Except that only two of us were genetically related, and one of us had a flexible nose disk and a hairy tail.

CHAPTER 5

A BLENDED FAMILY

CHURCH PROVED ANOTHER VALUABLE VENUE FOR SOLICITING SLOPS.

The minister was in on our scheme. "This is Sy Montgomery," he'd introduce me to new members and visitors in
hopes of securing edible garbage. "She lives with a pig. And
I'm not talking about her husband."

We did get some takers that way, but a more reliable
source of slops was the minister himself. Graham and his wife,
Maggie, would come over whenever they had a compost
buildup. Maggie adored Christopher and kept a photo of him
as a piglet on the window sill above the kitchen sink in the par-
sonage. That first summer we spent with Chris, Maggie had
started feeling sick from time to time, but she always felt bet-

ter around Christopher. And I always felt better around Maggie and Graham.

They were a little older than us, and both of them were scholars. Maggie had once been the dean of a women's college (though when Graham was called to our congregation she had to switch to waitressing at the local inn's restaurant). Graham had studied geology before switching to theology. Both of them read widely and thought deeply. Our discussions were always lively and sometimes profound—and often further stimulated by the edifying experience of watching a pig eat.

"One of the first things Jesus did was to drive demons out of a person and cast them into swine," Maggie remarked one day as Christopher chewed an overgrown zucchini she had brought from her garden. "I always thought that was no fair."

"Well, Jesus doesn't go around just being a nice guy," Graham said. "He's an exorcist. We forget this today. But the real problem with humans is, we're possessed with destructive spirits. So Jesus casts them into a herd of swine and sends them over a cliff."

"But what did the pigs do wrong?" I asked. "They were innocent bystanders. What did Jesus have against them?"

"Jesus probably hated pigs," Graham said.

I was stunned.

"This is a real challenge to my faith, Graham!"

The minister laughed. In his sermons, he often stressed the value of understanding the Bible in its historical and cultural context. Jesus, he pointed out, was, after all, a Jew living in Israel under Roman rule—a time, place, and culture where swine were considered vile, filthy animals.

Why this prejudice against pigs?

It could have simply been practical. Maggie (a superb cook, with whom I often swapped recipes) suggested that possibly the taboo against pork was a divinely inspired health ordinance. Eating undercooked pork carries the threat of trichinosis. The Koran, too, forbids the eating of pork, possibly for the same reason. (But actually you can get trichinosis from any insufficiently cooked meat.)

It could have been ecological. In *The Sacred Cow and the Abominable Pig,* the controversial anthropologist Marvin Harris argues that pigs were once popular meat animals in the Middle East (and in fact new data suggest that one of two subspecies of wild pigs from which all farm pigs arose was first domesticated there). But the Israel of Leviticus was no place for swine. By then, human overpopulation had destroyed Israel's Neolithic forests of oak and beech to make way for planted crops, especially olive groves. Without free forage, pigs were too expensive to raise—especially since, unlike sheep, goats, and cows, pigs can't provide their people with wool or milk. So Jewish lawmakers said, quite literally, to hell with them.

Graham and I have continued this conversation about religious taboos on pigs for fifteen years now. Recently he suggested yet another possibility. Perhaps pigs reminded the ancient Jews too much of ourselves. "Pigs are so close to humans," he said. "They're quite intelligent. Their hearts are so like ours that we use their valves in medicine. Their flesh even tastes like ours—or so I've heard." (I had, too. This fact inspired certain Polynesian cannibals to coin a term for Westerners who literally came for dinner: "long pig.")

"That may name our uneasiness with pigs," Graham said. "There's a sense that they're too close to home, as though we are eating an element of ourselves."

Shortly after this talk I read a passage suggesting the Jewish prohibition against pigs was paradoxical. In his classic *The Golden Bough,* James George Frazer writes that pigs may have been originally *venerated* by the Jews. Until the time of Isaiah, he suggests, Jews considered both mice and pigs divine, their flesh eaten during sacramental ceremonies, in the spirit that Christians eat the Eucharist, the body of Christ, today. The very fact that pigs are now so reviled suggests they were once revered, and that overturning the old order required vehement injunctions.

This could well be. For many cultures have—wisely, in my view—embraced the pig as a potent symbol of divinity.

For their strength and cunning, wild pigs were emulated by warriors, invoked by wizards, consulted by soothsayers. In pre-Christian Europe, fortune-tellers looked into the fresh livers of pigs to see the future, for it was said their organs reflected the divine rays sent down by the gods. In Mycenaean Greece, the brave and ferocious wild boar was sacred to Ares, the god of war. Throughout Europe and Asia, gods were often associated with boars; in many myths, gods are slain by boars, as people surely were. Sows were revered for their fecundity. A white sow was the symbol of the Welsh goddess Cerridwen, a lunar deity worshiped as the Great Mother. Wild pigs were the favorite animals of the fertility god Freyr and his sister, Freyja, to whom Norsemen and Anglo-Saxons made solemn sacrifices. As a baby, Zeus, the future chief of the Olympian gods, was suckled by a sow.

The Chinese consider the pig lucky, a symbol of both fertility and wealth. Even today, children collect their savings in ceramic piggy banks, perhaps a nod to the wisdom of a culture whose sterling accomplishments include domesticating pigs nine thousand years ago (a separate strain from the Middle Eastern stock) and inventing ceramics. In China, it is said that the Heavenly Jade Emperor himself named the twelfth year of the lunar calendar after the pig, for this was the twelfth creature to cross the finish line in a divinely inspired race to which all the animals were invited. People who are born in the Year of the Pig are believed to be blessed with the porcine qualities of sincerity, honesty, and kindness. (Consulting the place mat in a Chinese restaurant, I was disappointed to see that, unlike such lucky souls as Albert Schweitzer, Julie Andrews, and Ralph Waldo Emerson, neither Howard nor I—nor Christopher!—was born in a Pig year.)

Elsewhere in Asia, pigs are widely admired. A Hindu creation legend tells us the great god Vishnu took the form of a boar in order to lift up the Earth on his strong back from the waters of the primeval flood; he is often depicted with a boar's head on a human body. In Papua New Guinea, many tribes measure their wealth by the number of pigs they have. Women sometimes suckle orphaned pigs along with their own infants. In some of these areas, the pigs are not eaten. Instead they are admired for their beauty and fecundity, and especially for their handsome, curving tusks.

By the end of his first year with us, Christopher was yet to grow tusks. But already he was, I thought, very beautiful: his black and white coat glossy, his eyes bright and expressive, his black hooves shiny and trim. But his beauty was more than skin (or even lard) deep. Though we didn't realize it at the time, Christopher was already bringing to us the blessings for which pigs have been credited for centuries: strength, luck, friends, and even family.

A HOME OF OUR OWN, MEANINGFUL WORK, A GOOD MARRIAGE, friends we loved, a popular pig. What else could we want? Only one thing: a dog.

Actually we had tried to adopt a dog the summer that Chris was a piglet. On an errand to the A&P, Howard had seen an oak tag poster with photos advertising a two-year-old female border collie needing a good home. We'd watched these wonderful herding dogs working sheep on trips to New

Zealand and Great Britain and were enthralled with them. Howard saw that the phone number bore a nearby exchange, and called the minute he got home. But, to our disappointment, the lady who answered—Evelyn Naglie, who apparently ran a private humane shelter—was reluctant to let the dog go.

She explained that Tess, as the dog was named, had been brought in the previous winter by a family who found the border collie too rambunctious. Shortly after she arrived at Evelyn's, Tess had been in a terrible accident. Chasing a ball that a child had carelessly tossed into the street, she was hit by a snowplow, crushing her pelvis. She'd had two operations and had to live in a crate for much of the past year. Her right leg would never be the same.

Despite the promising poster, Tess really hadn't recovered enough to leave, Evelyn said. Howard asked her to keep our number and to call us when Tess was ready for adoption. But we never heard from her again.

A year later, on an August afternoon, our tenant Mary Pat told us she had some good news. She knew we were anxious to adopt a dog, especially since our beloved cat, Mika, had died of cancer in November. It turned out that the place where Mary Pat and John boarded their fluffy white Samoyed puppy, Chloe, also placed homeless animals. A border collie had just come in for adoption.

Howard called the number. A familiar voice answered. It was Evelyn. The border collie was a female, she said, three years old.

It was Tess.

We were meant to be together. We drove over to get Tess that afternoon.

. . .

BORDER COLLIES ARE DOGS WHO SHOULD COME WITH A WARNING label.

Tess's first family, we later learned, had made the mistake of adopting a border collie puppy and then leaving her alone in the house, frustrated, frightened, and bored. They would return to discover the puppy had destroyed everything in the house.

No wonder. Border collies are too smart and too intense to be left alone all day with nothing to do. If they have nothing to do, they will think of something—and probably not what you had in mind.

Border collies are bred not for looks but for brains. Border collies don't look like Lassie. They don't even always look like other border collies. They are usually black with a white blaze down the nose, a white ruff, and white at the tip of the tail. The ears can be floppy or pointed, the coat shaggy or short. The border collie was developed to herd sheep, often far from the shepherd, on the mountains and moors of the British Isles—a task requiring extraordinary agility, endurance, and intelligence. What distinguishes border collies is their outlook on life. They need meaningful work or they go crazy. Whether that work is herding sheep or chasing Frisbees, border collies are compulsive perfectionists, and do everything with incredible intensity and dedication.

Some call them maniacal.

The drive to herd is so powerful that, lacking sheep, border collies will herd squirrels, children, buses, even insects. They are exceptionally independent, emotional, and willful. In competitions, if the shepherd makes a mistake that costs them the ribbon, the dog might hold it against him for days. And border collies are so brilliant that they can figure out just about anything. They instantly understand how to open cabinets, doors, and refrigerators. One border collie (Devon from Jon

Katz's delightful *A Dog Year*) routinely broke out of his picket fence by systematically testing for one loose slat—and then always pushed it closed after the escape. He was also known to unwrap Katz's ham and cheese sandwich and carefully remove and eat only the ham, leaving the rest of the sandwich pristine.

I wondered—briefly—if adding another potentially diabolical genius to the household was really a good idea.

After all, just that week, our pig had been in police custody again.

I'd been in the "big city" of Keene (well, it was a city, anyway), a forty-minute drive away, teaching a short writing course at Antioch New England Graduate School. I'd let Chris out on his tether, and asked Howard to periodically check on him. The first check, he didn't see the pig, but saw his rope, leading downhill into a mud wallow among some trees, was taut. Second check, the rope was in the exact same position. Howard followed the rope. There was no pig at the end.

Howard ran down Route 137 shaking a coffee can full of grain. Mike Cass came up the street to meet him.

"Looking for something?" Mike asked.

"Yeah," replied Howard, "About two hundred fifty pounds of back bacon."

But Ed already had Chris in custody and was leading him back to our barn with apples.

The next night the pig was on TV. He'd made a cameo appearance on New Hampshire Public Television, in a segment filmed at our house by a local producer, Liz Klein. The show was ostensibly about my book, *Walking with the Great Apes,* which had been published that spring. The show had interviews with me and clips of Jane Goodall, Dian Fossey, and Biruté Galdikas. But what everyone remembered was the shot of Christopher eagerly trotting behind me down to his Pig Plateau, trailed by the chickens.

"Saw your pig on TV," Mike said to Howard when they next met at the Cash Market.

"Yes," Howard replied, "one day he's a convicted felon, the next day he's on TV."

"Isn't America great?" Mike said.

WE WORRIED. WOULD TESS RUN AWAY? WOULD SHE BARK INCESsantly? Would she chase the chickens? And most upsetting of all, would she try to herd the pig? (This wouldn't go over with Chris, we were sure.)

But she did none of these things. She ignored the other animals. She was entirely and obsessively focused on us.

Things went astonishingly well at first. The moment we got her to her new home, we first spent some time playing with her favorite tennis ball in the yard. Howard would toss, and Tess ran after it like the wind. Unless you watched her very carefully, you would never suspect the weakness in her right rear leg. She leaped into the air—all four legs off the ground— seized the ball in her jaws, and then whipped back to us, spitting the toy into our outstretched hands. Although Howard had by far the better arm, Tess brought it back to me every other time. She was keeping track. We played until her tongue was hanging out.

It then occurred to us that Tess should probably empty her bladder before coming into the house. I led her into the tall grass of the field. "Tess, pee," I suggested, not particularly hopeful that anything would happen—but to my amazement, she squatted and took care of the matter instantly. "Good dog!" It was not so much praise, but a statement of fact.

"Tess, come," we said as we invited her to the house. She followed us intently. And from there she commenced surveying our every move with her intense brown eyes, applying her considerable intellect to figuring out what Howard and I wanted her to do.

She would sit beside one of us for thirty minutes, keeping me or Howard in the laserlike focus of her stare as if it were some sort of tractor beam. Then she might switch to the other person. By the time an hour passed, we could feel the buildup of tension. We went outside to toss the tennis ball or Frisbee again. She was a Gold Glover, Howard said. She caught and retrieved anything you tossed with the same intensity, grace, and skill. But although Tess enjoyed catching the toys, we felt that to her, this wasn't play. It was work—work she loved— and she took it quite as seriously as we did ours. Perhaps she felt if she impressed us enough with her catching, we would let her stay.

Although her energy was frenetic, in other ways Tess was heartbreakingly reserved. She merely tolerated our petting her. She did not kiss us, sit at our feet, beg for food at the table, or solicit affection as other dogs do. She was too elegant and refined for that. But she did not want to be alone. Not even outside.

After we heard her whole story from Evelyn, we understood why. Tess's first family couldn't cope with her energy, Evelyn said. Any family foolish enough to adopt a border collie puppy and then leave her at home alone all day couldn't have possibly understood how to lovingly house-train an animal—even one as smart as a border collie. When Tess predictably destroyed the house, the family punished her. And then she was abandoned. At least the family had the good sense to place her with Evelyn. But next came her terrible accident, followed by two operations and a prolonged, painful recovery.

When finally Tess had recovered enough to adopt her out, Evelyn had lost our phone number and forgotten all about us.

A retired couple had phoned later, and Tess went to live with them. They had loved her, and she had loved them. At last she had a home. But this lasted only one brief year. The couple lost their house in the recession. They had to move to a cheap, dog-free apartment. Reluctantly, they brought Tess back to Evelyn. And then finally, thanks to Mary Pat, Tess had come home with us.

She was understandably wary of her new family. When we patted the couch to invite her to sit with us, she stared at us in disbelief. When she finally hopped up, she seemed torn between fear of disobeying our command and fear she might be scolded for doing something that clearly had not been allowed before. When we invited her to sleep in our bed, she was incredulous. Tense, she would stand on the futon hesitantly, then leap down at the first opportunity, as if she expected us to shoo her away. She would eat her food only if we praised her lavishly afterward—"You ate your food! Oh, good dog! What a dog! Tess is so good!"—and then gave her a biscuit for dessert.

That whole first week we had her, she didn't once bark. Then the Fed Ex man came. (Howard was a proponent of the theory that dogs bark at delivery people believing that otherwise these shifty characters would *take* something *away* from your house. But because dogs bark, they *leave* something instead—a sequence of events that proves to dogs that their barking is indeed effective.) When Tess issued a series of arfs, we praised her as if this were the most inspired and original thing any dog had ever done.

She didn't chew things, either. And for her loo, she used the tall grass in the back field—not the lawn and never the house—but she didn't even dare pee unless we asked her. It was as if she felt that we, her third family, were her last chance, and she didn't want to blow it. But it also seemed as if she was always formulating a contingency plan in case we didn't work out. She seemed to be guarding her emotions, protecting her heart from being broken once again.

In bringing Tess home, we realized, we had taken on a monumental, lifetime commitment: we had to earn the love of this fiercely intelligent, beautiful, and mysterious creature. It was up to us to redeem the cruelty and sorrow of her past.

Between Chris and Tess and the Ladies, Howard and I were now not only outnumbered but outsmarted—not to mention outweighed. What did we think we were doing?

Some people consider their animals their substitute children. Certain psychologists explain away the loving relationships between people and animals in terms of thwarted parenthood. These psychologists have identified a group of physical traits, such as the flat face and big eyes of pug dogs, that they call "baby releasers," and claim the sight of these activate a torrent of misplaced maternal feelings toward animals. This suggests that any friendship between a human and an animal is really just some kind of wiring mistake, a person's thwarted yearning for a human infant—a simpleminded view that, in my opinion, insults mothers, diminishes animals, and underestimates the complexity of love.

Our animals were not our babies. True, Howard and I had raised Chris as a piglet—but there was no mistaking him for a baby anything now. By his first birthday, Christopher Hogwood was big enough to eat us. (That was another reason we didn't give him meat—we didn't want to give him ideas.) Our chickens were no longer babies, either (as their eighty eggs a week proved); they were adults, as we were. And no one could have mistaken Tess for anything other than an adult. She was a fully formed, mature creature with a mysterious past of her own.

No, our animals were no babies. Besides, if we had wanted babies, we knew full well how to get them. But we chose not to.

Not wanting children is something many people don't understand. "Don't you feel your womb calling to you?" a woman acquaintance my age asked me. I replied that my organs seldom had much to say, and that I hoped things would stay that way. In fact, I was more adamant about staying child-free than Howard was. In our mid-twenties, he had broached the subject of children—once. My sensitive, wifely reply was something like: "Forget it." I had nixed the idea of having children when I was myself a child, having learned in the 1960s that human overpopulation was literally crowding other species off the planet. Why create another mouth to gnaw at the overburdened earth? I was about seven years old at the time and have never for a moment regretted the decision.

I never went crazy for babies the way a lot of other girls did. Babies would have been far more appealing to me if they had fur, like most normal mammals. Other mammals whose young are this naked wisely tuck their babies into holes, or if they happen to be marsupials such as possums or kangaroos, keep them hidden in a pouch, until they are cute and furry enough for public viewing. I didn't hate babies, of course. But having made my decision, I never nurtured a desire to produce one. So when I found myself happily married, fulfilled in my work, and surrounded with friends of many species, children were simply not part of the picture.

Until the day two blond-haired girls came pouring over the stone wall next door, drawn irresistibly to a black and white spotted pig.

STANDING IN A COLD, EMPTY HOUSE, THE FORLORN LITTLE GIRLS and their mother wanted only one thing: to go home. But they couldn't. That was the very problem that brought them to the vacant house next door.

They were still reeling from the divorce. It had taken four years and three lawyers to end Lilla Cabot's marriage to the girls' father. The worst of it was that now, Kate, ten, and Jane, seven, were being forced to give up the home where they had lived all their lives.

Kate and Jane had loved the little shingle-style cottage in the middle of Hancock's deepest woods. It was near the nature center, surrounded by hundreds of acres of protected land. There, the sisters had learned the songs of chickadees and the drummings of woodpeckers, where to find salamanders, how to catch frogs. The cottage had been in the family since Lilla's great-great-grandfather built it. But now the house had to be sold.

At the time, New Hampshire, as well as the rest of the nation, was in the grip of a recession. Though money was tight, the local real estate market was hot. The day the divorce came through, the house sold within three hours of going on the market.

Now, Lilla and her daughters had to find a place to live—fast. The old house next door to us was the only one available for rent in town that would let them move in by January. The kids hated it instantly. Kate and Jane had never even been in an empty house before. It felt creepy. It was October, and already it was obvious the place had no insulation. "It was so uninviting," Kate remembers. "One of those dark, old, run-down little houses that's colder inside than out."

But they had no choice. In January, two other girls would be moving in to *their* house. Kate and Jane thought sadly of the other girls' dolls and dollhouses spread over the beloved old rooms where Kate and Jane had played with their stuffed animals—the big black and white orca whale and the howling

Arctic wolf and the black panther. The sisters felt betrayed, and these cold, empty rooms were the very embodiment of how they felt inside.

With their mom, they walked outside, miserable. They wandered into their backyard.

Then Kate saw something big and black and white next door.

"Can we look? Can we look?" the girls asked their mother. Kate, who like her younger sister was enthralled by horses, had noticed the barn next door and thought maybe there was a pony. They took off, Kate first, Jane following.

Just as she leaped over the stone wall that separated the two properties, Kate saw Christopher's face.

"Wow!" she said to her sister. "This is even cooler than a horse! It's a *pig!*"

From the Pig Plateau, Christopher, Tess, and I looked up to see two beautiful little blond girls running toward us. Chris flexed his nose disk to catch their scent and uttered a grunt. "Come over and meet Christopher Hogwood!" I said. "And this is Tess . . ."

I didn't ask who they were, and I didn't introduce myself. We got right down to business.

"Sure, you can pet him! Here, feel behind his ears!"

"It's so soft back there!"

"He's got so much hair!"

"I thought pigs were pink. . . ."

"Now, watch this," I said, sure to impress our audience: "You rub his tummy, right over his nipples, like this—look at all the excellent nipples he has! That's right . . . stand back, he's going to go over. . . ."

Christopher got that dreamy look in his eyes, dropped to his knees, and then rolled on his side, landing with a thud.

"Oh!" the girls gasped in unison.

"Unh!" answered Christopher. "Unn-n-n-n-h-h-h-h . . ."

"He wants us to keep rubbing," I said. But Chris had already made this obvious, grunting in ecstasy in time to the rhythm of their little hands. "Wow—he really likes you both!"

Lilla, a thirty-six-year-old version of her golden-haired, blue-eyed daughters, crossed over the low stone wall to survey the scene: her girls, surrounded by eight curious hens and tended by a suspicious border collie, were completely absorbed in the task of petting and massaging a blissful, supine, black-and-white 250-pound hog.

"The moment I saw him," Lilla remembers, "the cloud of anxiety and despair around our little unit just lifted away. The sensation went all over my body: *everything's going to be all right.*"

Our four blond heads now bent intently forward as eight hands reached to rub Chris's pink, tight belly. Keeping time with his grunts, we repeated his favorite mantra:

"Good, good pig. Good, good, goood . . ."

CHAPTER 6

PIG SPA

"OK — I'm opening the door. Are you ready?"

Kate and Jane stood by, just off to one side of the barn and slightly uphill—a direction in which Chris was unlikely to run.

"OK!" they answered. "Ready!"

The girls knew the drill. By Christopher's second year, we had perfected the Running of the Pig. We'd done this nearly every day that the sky had shown the least hint of sunshine and the ground was clear of snow. By now, it was a regular ritual, and its smooth operation depended on the girls' well-honed execution of their tasks.

One: Slops Standby. I would carry the heavy bucket, but at least one of the girls—usually both—stood ready with a particularly delectable item, such as a blueberry muffin or a bagel, with which to steer Chris if he went off course.

Two: Wardrobe Management. Christopher had outgrown the extra-large dog harness, and now dressed for dinner in a more elaborate contraption we had to put on him after he exited the pen. It was an amalgam of previous outfits. At one point he'd worn a harness that we'd had custom-made by a manufacturer of spelunking gear, generously procured by Maggie and Graham's daughter, Emily, who was dating a caver. But—disturbingly—it *broke*. So this became the substrate onto which bits of earlier harnesses were cleverly grafted, thanks to the skill and ingenuity of the only cobbler for miles around—a fellow whose shop was a half-hour drive away. (Chris was his only sixteen-toed client.) Kate, a fourth-grade fashion maven, carried the harness, and was the only one of us who could consistently negotiate the maze of buckles and loops necessary to put the thing on.

Three: Border (Collie) Patrol. Jane helped me make sure that Tess, who, with her Frisbee, accompanied us on every trip we made outside for any reason, maintained her "stay" well afield of Christopher's trajectory until the coast was clear. This was not as easy as it sounds. Even after a year with us, Tess was unconvinced we might not slip away from her. So whenever we were more than a few yards apart, Tess tried to creep ever closer to me unseen—even though once I gave the "stay" command she was invariably crouched down, immobile, every time I looked up. With Tess focused on me, and Chris on the slops I carried, an unwitting collision of the two animals was entirely possible—but for Jane. Jane's attention was unwavering. Though she was only seven and short for her age, Jane's sturdy determination was evident in everything she did, from her focused ferocity on the first-grade soccer team to the way she herded her free-spirited mom and older sister out the door so they would not be hopelessly late for every appointment. She was perfect for the job.

Lastly, there was a fourth task, unstated but clearly understood: don't get run over by the pig. We all knew this could pose a serious problem, because by the second summer of his life, Christopher Hogwood weighed well over three hundred pounds.

A three-hundred-pound pig in the family seemed perfectly normal to me. Having children in my life, though, came as a huge surprise.

Even for a childless couple, Howard and I had remarkably little contact with kids. Howard's brother and sister-in-law had two fine sons, Eric and Scott, but they lived on Long Island and we seldom saw them. The friends with whom we spent the most time were older, their children grown—or they were child-free like us. Writing, as we did, for adult readers didn't bring us in contact with many kids; our civic duties (I served on the conservation commission and as a deaconess at church, and Howard chaired the library's board of trustees) didn't, either.

Which was fine with me. I'd never been one of those people who was "good with kids"—not even when I was a kid myself.

My childhood playmates were mainly adult. Our Scottish terrier, Molly, and I had been pups together, but all the others—the parakeets and box turtles, fish and lizards—were grown when I met them. As for young humans, I knew little about them. When we'd lived at Fort Hamilton, I didn't go to school with the other kids on base. Weekdays I rode into Brooklyn in a limousine to Packer Collegiate Institute, a private Protestant school with huge brass banisters coiling alongside curving wooden staircases, teachers who yelled if you put your elbows on the lunch table, and an hour of chapel every morning. My classmates lived too far away to play with regularly on weekends, and no kid on base wanted to play with the general's daughter.

But no matter. Outside, I didn't *want* to play kickball in the street, anyway; I wanted to walk with Molly and see what she was smelling. Indoors, I didn't *want* to play with other girls and their silly dolls; I preferred the prehistoric inhabitants of Purplenoiseville, a dinosaur village ruled by a battery-powered foot-tall purple and green tyrannosaur named King Zor, who rolled forward spitting sparks and rubber-tipped darts to keep the smaller brontosaurs, ankylosaurs, and ceratopsians in line. The dinosaurs were surprisingly devoted. Purplenoiseville had been settled when I was four and we lived in Alexandria, Virginia; I'd assumed that when we moved, since we couldn't take Alexandria with us, we couldn't take Purplenoiseville either. But one day shortly after the move to Fort Hamilton, the doorbell rang and I opened the door to find King Zor waiting on the doorstep. In the coming days, I would breathlessly report to my parents how, one by one, all the dinosaurs appeared, having journeyed all the way from Virginia to New York. If anyone had asked me at the time, I would have said I had plenty of friends.

By fifth grade, when my father retired from the Army and we moved to New Jersey, I was earning straight A's, had memorized the Methodist hymnal, and read French and English at a high school level. But I had no idea how to play with children. A quarter century later, I still hadn't learned.

But Christopher Hogwood changed everything.

FROM THE FIRST DAY THE CABOTS MOVED IN THAT JANUARY, a white, five-gallon plastic ice cream bucket dominated their kitchen counter. This was the slops bucket, the focus of every meal.

"Oooh—pasta!" the girls would cry in delight on a night Lilla made spaghetti. "Christopher would really like that!" The girls would eat just the tiniest bit for dinner in order to leave more for the pig's enjoyment.

"Bagels! Great!" they would exclaim at breakfast, making sure there were plenty of leftovers for the pig. At their house, burned cookies were cause for rejoicing, and when one day a whole watermelon splattered on the floor, the fallen fruit was greeted with a whoop of pleasure, as if a skilled basketball player had landed a slam-dunk . . . right into Christopher's pen.

When the family had moved in, I had told them to feel free to bring treats for Chris at any time, but to make sure to come see me first. Possibly Lilla thought this was a neighborly gesture to ensure her small daughters were not stepped on or bitten by an enormous hog. This was not the case. Actually my main concern was that no one fed Christopher anything unsavory. (People new to feeding pigs, I'd found, were apt to forget about Christopher's meat taboo or his dislike of onions and citrus, and might even carelessly toss a plastic wrapper or a toothpick into the pig garbage.)

The first afternoon after the girls moved in, they came bearing slops. I was deep in writing my monthly nature column for the *Boston Globe,* this time on what bugs do in winter. (Our house was a living laboratory of answers, with pupal cases and egg sacs in many corners, safe from my little-used vacuum cleaner.) As happened every time there was a knock at the door, Tess exploded into hysteria, shattering my concentration. Often she barked so loudly we couldn't hear the knocking that prompted it. But in this case I knew from her tone that something truly alarming was trying to get in the house: *children.*

Tess did not trust children. Perhaps they reminded her of unruly sheep. When I opened the door, she snapped her teeth in the girls' faces. A border collie's snap is not a bite that misses its mark; it's a gesture made specifically for the sound. It helps them herd sheep, like you might click your tongue to gee a horse along. Unfortunately most people don't know this—the children start to cry and the parents shrill in alarm.

But this is not what happened at all.

In response to Tess's assault, little Jane bravely stood her ground; Kate knelt to pat Tess: "Hello, Tess! Remember us?" (Tess probably did, but she also remembered Mary Pat and John, and still barked relentlessly every time our tenants entered or left the house, which was several times a day.) Over the din, Lilla tried to apologize for the interruption, and explained they'd only come to see if they could feed Christopher.

"Tess!" I barked, grabbing my ski jacket. "Get your Frisbee, Tess!" The tone of Tess's voice changed from hysterical to victorious. Thanks to her barking, instead of being abducted by aliens, we would now be able to play Frisbee. Remarkably still able to bark with the toy in her mouth, Tess flew down the icy back steps with the four of us, leaping into the air to grab the disk as we tossed it to her over the crusty snow on the way to the barn.

Christopher heard our footsteps and began to call to us: "Unhhhhhh? Nhhhhhhhhhhhhhh? Nhhhhhhhhhhhhhh!"

"Hello, Pig Man!" I answered. "Visitors!"

We rounded the corner to the barn.

"He's even bigger!"

"Look at his ears!"

"He's so furry!"

"Can I feed him?"

"Ooh, please, let *me*!"

The girls were hooked.

After school, right off the bus, the sisters would head straight for the pen and place their uneaten lunch sandwiches

Christopher Hogwood comes home—in front of our barn, as a baby.
Photo: Author

Even when he began to bulk up, at first, Chris stayed about the size of a cat.
Photo: Howard Mansfield

Quite early in life, Christopher began to probe his pen for a means of escape. *Photo: Howard Mansfield*

Off to the Pig Plateau...Chris, Tess (with Frisbee), and Sy (with slops bucket). Chris is about one and a half years old here. *Photo: Howard Mansfield*

Chris as a young adult wearing a large dog harness. Later, our cobbler friend would have to sew together the parts from several dog harnesses to accomodate Chris's girth.
Photo: Author

Christopher begins his career as a fashion model—this photo became the first Chris-mas card.
Photo: Bruce Curtis

The ladies spill out of their newly completed Chicken Chalet.
Photo: Pincus Mansfield

Chris as a young adult resting on the Pig Plateau and enjoying a belly rub
Photo: Ian Redmund

Tess soars to catch her beloved Frisbee. *Photo: Pincus Mansfield*

Antioch biology professor Beth Kaplan and her daughter Stella at Pig Spa
Photo: Author

This Christmas
card photo
showcased Chris's
tusks—before we
had to have them
trimmed.
Photo: Author

Sy and Jane with baby chicks, who arrived in the mail to supplement the ranks of the aging Ladies. *Photo: Howard Mansfield*

What is beer but liquid grain? Christopher enjoys a Schlitz. *Photo: Author*

Ned Rodat relaxes with Chris, an elder statesman at the time.
Photo: Mollie Miller

Christopher's last full summer, at age thirteen. Pig Spa with Kate (left)
and Jane. *Photo: Lilla Cabot*

Above: Christopher's last
Christmas card
Photo: Author

Christopher's gravesite
Photo: Jarvis Coffin

into the pig's mouth. "I don't know why I even pack their lunch," Lilla once joked with Howard. "I could just put it in the slops bucket right now."

The girls came up with the idea of feeding Christopher with a serving spoon. One day they decided that a half gallon of Häagen-Dazs was too freezer-burned for human consumption. Christopher shocked us all by launching from all fours to stand up on his back legs to receive the bounty. Resting his front legs on the gate, he brought his huge head level with Kate's—and towered above Jane's. He opened his cavernous mouth and awaited his due.

Interestingly, he seemed to understand the function of the spoon. Gently, he allowed the girls to slide it out from between his lips, even if a bit of ice cream remained on its surface: he was confident of refills. With what would pass for patience in a pig, he would wait, his trotters draped casually over the gate, for another spoonful, ropes of frothy drool flowing down his jowls.

Now, this was my idea of a good time.

Outside, there were also hens to pet, eggs to gather, Frisbees to throw. Soon the girls began to spend time with us inside, too. Their mom was commuting to Massachusetts on weekdays, earning a master's degree in expressive therapy at Lesley College. When Kate and Jane got home from school each day, their house was cold and empty—and once it was *haunted*. One day Kate and Jane came over screaming. The stereo, they said, had, "like, suddenly come on *for no reason?*— and then *Janis Joplin* was *singing? Like, really loud?*" Obviously the two-hundred-year-old cape was haunted by a troubled 1960s blues singer.

By then, though, the girls knew they were safe with us. After playing with Chris and Tess and the chickens, with eggs in our pockets, many afternoons we retreated to our tiny kitchen and made chocolate chip cookies together, baking them in the 1930s gas oven that warmed up the whole house. (We nearly always burned at least a few for Chris.) While I rolled out pie crusts on our single, three-foot-long countertop, the girls sat at the rickety card table where Howard and I ate, and drank milk with the cookies and talked.

At first, we mainly spoke of Christopher. How many different grunts did he have, and what did they mean? They identified the "Come over!" grunt, the "Feed me faster!" grunt, the "Let me out!" grunt, the "Rub more!" grunt, and an endless variety of others, including Christopher's special grunt for Howard: the deep, serious, "man-to-man" grunt. (And these were just the grunts. He also uttered growls, squeals, and snorts as well as a blood-chilling alarm bark.) Which foods hadn't Christopher tried yet? What might appeal to him? What had he been like as a baby?

I showed them his baby pictures. They could not believe he was once so small.

We discussed other species of pigs. I showed them the pictures of the babirusa and red river hog. They pronounced them gorgeous. Together we admired the bearded pigs of Indonesia, the cute peccaries of the Americas. Sometimes we talked about other animals around the world—orcas and wolves, elephants and monkeys. We would pick a category—weasels, for instance—and everyone would name their favorite animal among them. Wolverines, we decided, were very cool. But ferrets were, too. And otters were excellent. We looked up the animals' pictures and read aloud from my volumes of *Walker's Mammals of the World* and the Torstar Books series All the World's Animals, while our cockatiel chewed on the pages or flew from head to head.

Attracted by the smell of baking cookies, Howard would descend from his upstairs office. He was working on a book about New Hampshire aviator Harry Atwood, famous for his daring 1911 landing on the White House lawn. (President Taft waddled out to give Atwood a medal but was too fat to accept the invitation to fly.) Often Howard would eat cookies with us and then go next door and build a fire in the woodstove, so that when Lilla got home, the house wouldn't be so cold.

We called their home the Doll House. It was a small, sweet place, with a picket fence out front where roses bloomed in the summer and the rooms inside always smelled of bubble bath. With the Lillas Three in residence—the girls were exact miniatures of their slender, pretty mom—the house next door was a feminine universe, fragrant with fruity shampoos and exotic hand creams, littered with little girls' gloves and scarves and hair scrunchies, colorful with grade school artwork on the refrigerator and crystals and suncatchers in the windows. Sometimes we would join them over there and eat pizza. Jane would hop up and dance on the chair in front of the woodstove until her pants were really hot, then she'd eat an ice cube to cool off. Kate ran up and down the stairs, bringing us her drawings and poetry and stuffed animals.

One Sunday we went on an expedition together. Kate and Jane had wanted to visit George and Mary's ever since they'd seen Christopher's baby pictures. And as winter's snow melted into mud season, surely there would be baby pigs.

It was a merry journey, Kate and Jane chattering and giggling nonstop in the backseat. On the drive over to the farm, as we rounded the bend known as Cemetery Cove that curves around the lake, the girls cried, "Jack rabbit!" and held their breath until the first white house they saw. Why? They didn't know. (Howard did: "Because," he explained, "they're seven and ten.")

When we arrived, we went right to the barn. The baby pigs were all in with their huge moms—there were no stalls set aside for runts, as when Chris had been born. The girls leaned over the gates to the stalls until they were hanging like gymnasts with their legs up and their heads down, reaching to pet the babies. Kate was desperate to hold a baby pig. Normally Howard and I would have gone right in, but the possibility, though slight, that one of the girls might be injured by one of George's sweet, huge sows scared us. Instead, we urged the girls to explore the muddy barnyard, where they found rabbits and chickens to hold. As they picked them up, the animals became calm in their hands.

But Kate was disappointed. She had really wanted to hold a baby pig.

As we were leaving, George appeared as if from nowhere. He looked like a caricature of a man late to a fire, running as fast as he could, carrying a bucket in one callused, ungloved hand. One of his draft horses was loose, he called to us as he ran by. It might be halfway to Keene by now.

"George, we'll catch up later . . . you go!" Howard and I told him.

But then Kate, whom George had never met, called after him plaintively, "We wanted to hold a baby pig. . . ."

George stopped in his tracks. He set down the bucket. He opened the gate to a maternity stall, picked out two pink piglets, and handed one to Kate and one to Jane. Then he ran off and reappeared with a half gallon of maple syrup for Howard and me. Finally he put the piglets back in the stall—and then took up the bucket and continued his high-speed chase after the loose draft horse.

THE VISIT TO GEORGE AND MARY'S SIGNALED THE END OF ONE OF New Hampshire's fiercer winters. At our house, as Christopher slept snug in his bed of hay, and hens roosted warm in their nest boxes, our upstairs windows frosted over, so we could see only out of a one-inch porthole. Tess, Howard, and I huddled close together in our bed. Some nights the wind howled so loudly our walls seemed to sigh. But it was much worse next door. At night, Kate and Jane could see their breaths in their uninsulated upstairs bedrooms. One night, snow piled on Jane's bed from a broken skylight. To try to warm up before bed, the girls would take hot showers and then burrow under the covers. The damp bath towels would be frozen stiff by morning.

For the girls, the winter had been difficult in other ways, too. Fourth grade was Kate's first in public school—like me, she'd gone to a private school, and she found the transition to a public one difficult. It was hard to fit in. Her schoolwork was frustrating, especially because Kate had dyslexia. And the whole family had problems with the girls' father.

But they had a way to cope. I didn't know it at the time, but the younger Lillas would do exactly what I did when I needed to cry: go to Christopher's pen. At these times, he did not demand food. He grunted softly as we confided our private troubles and scratched his ears. In his huge presence, our sorrows somehow felt smaller.

The old house, as it turned out, was just as cold as everyone had feared it would be. But because of Chris, the move was not nearly as lonely.

The hens were the first to realize the change that had occurred. At some point that winter, Howard and I noticed they had begun hopping over the low stone wall that separated ours from the yard next door. As far as the Ladies were concerned, they, Christopher, Tess, Howard, Lilla, I, and the two girls had become one unit.

. . .

"OK!" I would say when everyone was ready. At this point in the Running of the Pig, Christopher would be bellowing in anticipation, rocking the gate violently with his nose.

I'd slide back the bolt, swing open the door, and shout, *"Go!"*

Christopher surged out of his pen, bucking and snorting. Any chickens in the way burst like grouse from cover and flew off in all directions. I ran ahead like a madwoman, struggling with the main slops bucket to get to the Plateau before Chris. The girls brought up the rear, as fast as their legs would carry them.

Christopher was young and powerful—a speeding pig bullet. I think he felt his strength and youth all the more in the limelight of our admiration. He enjoyed putting on a show. Watching a three-hundred-pound beast charge at top speed "was just a little bit scary," Jane admitted later—"and that made it exhilarating." It was all part of a game. Even as we ran, we could see that Chris looked each one of us in the eye, as if to make sure we were playing our parts.

Three pairs of pounding boots, sixty-four scaly chicken toes, and four thundering hooves all raced toward the finish line at the Pig Plateau and its rewards. There was a prize for everyone. Chris would receive his beloved slops. While he was communing with his Higher Power, Tess would rise from her "stay" for play with the Frisbee. The hens, too, got treats. They darted in to seize morsels from the edges of Christopher's slops pile, then raced back out of range, their beaks trailing carrot peelings and spaghetti.

And then, if the day was sunny and the weather fine, came the best part of the whole operation. After Christopher had eaten his fill, as Tess's tongue hung out from catching and re-trieving the Frisbee, after the hens had stolen enough scraps to turn their attention to the bugs in the taller grass of the field, came the main event of our summer days.

It was an activity that Kate and Jane perfected, one that eventually became a summer institution that drew children to the Pig Plateau in Hancock for a dozen years. We called it Pig Spa.

None of us can remember the specific moment the girls made the leap of imagination that transformed plain old tummy-rubbing into Pig Spa. But we are fairly sure the inspiration was Christopher's tail.

Like all the parts of our pig, his tail was extraordinary. It never achieved the tight curl of picture-book pigs, but Christopher Hogwood's back end nonetheless ended with a great flourish: the coarse white hair on his tail grew nearly a foot beyond the fleshy tip, and it cascaded to the ground in a thick, appealing ringlet.

At least it had been appealing the previous fall. Winter is hard on a pig's tail. There are many days in winter when a pigpen simply can't be cleaned. You can't push a wheelbarrow to the compost pile through deep snow (though there were days we loaded piles of manure on a sled we had found at the dump). But some days, everything you'd want to move is frozen solid anyway. When it does begin to warm up, the opportunities for a long tail to trail into softening slopsicles and melting manure are myriad. By spring, Christopher Hogwood's magnificent tail was a mess: matted, tangled, and embedded with detritus.

To two little girls, the ruined ringlet begged for a beauty treatment.

Most animals would prefer that people leave their tails

alone. Tess was one of them. She hated having her tail brushed and sat on it whenever she saw me carrying her red brush. From my earliest pony rides with my father, I had learned not to mess with a horse's back end, either, for fear of getting kicked. Even touching the tail of a snake (who you can argue *is* mostly one long tail) will usually cause the animal to turn around and face you with suspicion and then slither off.

How would our three-hundred-pound pig react to two little girls combing the tangles from his tail?

Christopher loved it.

Out of the Doll House came the perfect detangling devices: a lilac-colored brush with plastic bristles tipped with little white balls (they were intended to protect the scalp from scratches) and a dark blue comb with widely spaced teeth. Christopher particularly enjoyed it when the grooming extended to the hefty cheeks of his butt. He would often move a hind leg forward in order to show you exactly the spot that needed attention.

Occasionally, the comb would pull. Christopher would flick his tail in annoyance. If you persisted, and he didn't like it, he would pull his huge head off the ground and growl. But discomfort would be forgotten if you rubbed his belly or touched his ear and reassured him. "Good, good pig . . . Good, good, good." He closed his eyes and his whole body would heave with grunts of contentment.

Tail combing was just the beginning. The girls decreed that the tail would also, of course, need to be braided. And once it got warm enough, Christopher would need a bath. We quickly learned that temperature was crucial to the success of this endeavor. Although the garden hose would have made our job easy, that wouldn't do: the water came from our well and was too cold. Chris leaped up shrieking as if we were trying to butcher him. No, instead we had to carry heavy buckets of warm, soapy water from the kitchen, and then buckets of warm water for the rinse. We had to do this while he was lying down, so the aesthetic effect of the bath was somewhat diminished: one side of him would be squeaky clean, the other side lying in soapy mud. And of course if we managed to get him to stand up and convince him to lie down again the other way so we could wash his flip side, the side we'd just cleaned got all muddy.

Soon our simple comb and brush would be augmented with other beauty products. At the Blue Seal feed store, I bought a jar of The Hoofmaker, a fragrant, creamy concoction of cocoa butter mixed with something else and guaranteeing shiny, healthy hooves for show horses. We rubbed this into Christopher's hooves till they gleamed. We bought three kinds of scrub brushes with bristles of varied stiffnesses to accommodate the varying sensitivities of Christopher's skin. (His back and rear could take vigorous brushing, but as you got closer to his head he demanded, with a growl, softer bristles.)

Pig skin is so like a person's that skin from hogs is sometimes used as a temporary graft for human victims of massive burns. (The pig skin stays on for days or weeks, as the person's own skin heals, before the graft is ultimately rejected.) So no wonder Christopher's was vulnerable to the same problems as ours: sunburn, dermatitis, eczema. Happily, pig skin responds well to human skin care products. You just have to buy huge amounts. At one point, later in Christopher's life, Howard ordered a gallon of cod liver oil (Where do you find *a gallon* of cod liver oil? At Codliveroil.com) to keep his skin supple. He drank some of it—he *liked* it—but we found it worked best rubbed directly on his skin. And many years later, when Christopher was so old that he exhibited what we called porcine pattern baldness, our vet prescribed summer baths with a special foaming antiseptic soap. We would follow this treatment with a rubdown with Vitamin E skin cream with aloe.

To some, this beauty regimen might sound over the top for a pig. But the truth is, while the brushing, bathing, tail braiding, and nipple stroking delighted Christopher Hogwood, even more it restored the humans who touched him.

Word spread. Kate and Jane began to bring their friends to Pig Spa. I invited professors at the grad school where I sometimes taught to bring their kids. Deacons from church came with grandchildren. The Amidons brought their grandchildren from Iowa—a place with no shortage of pigs. But they had never seen a pig like this. All the little visitors were thrilled.

But besides Kate and Jane, the kid who loved him most was Kelly Felgar.

Kelly's mom, Amy, heard about Chris at the post office, a place where you can usually count on interesting and varied conversation with your neighbors. "The topic of cantaloupe rinds came up," Amy told me, "and then Pat Soucy mentioned saving slops for Chris. Kelly would *love* to meet Christopher! She adores pigs!"

I knew the Felgars from church, but I had never suspected their radiant, blue-eyed twelve-year-old was a pig-lover. All I knew about Kelly was that she had cancer.

The Felgars had moved to town from Athens, Georgia, when Kelly's dad became CEO of our local hospital. Back then Kelly was eight, and when she first saw the tiny elementary school on Main Street she said, "That's not a school—that's a house!" But any qualms she'd had about moving to a small, rural community were quelled on their first visit to the

Friendly Farm, a modest area attraction whose motto was "See 'em, feed 'em, pet 'em." There she fell in love with a mother pig lying on her side, nursing a row of pink piglets. She adored babies, and she loved that they were nursing (her mom, Amy, was a leader at La Leche League). And the scene reminded Kelly of the summer she and her older brother, Adam, used to play with a two-foot-long black-and-white pig named Miss Piggy who lived on her grandmother's farm.

Shortly after that, Kelly began amassing her pig collection: A pig-pile figurine carved from ivory-colored material. A pig puzzle carved from wood. Pigs of metal and plastic. Sleeping pigs and suckling pigs. A pig ballerina dancing on tiptoe (but then, pigs are always on tiptoe) clad in a pink tutu. She slept with a plushy brown pig with a squishy nose that squeaked.

Collecting pigs was just one of Kelly's hobbies; she also sang in the choir at church, won ribbons in figure skating competitions, and loved to dance. But after her diagnosis, and the brain surgery and radiation that followed, some days she didn't feel well enough to do these other things. Tending the pigs in her room was a reliable source of joy. One summer, Howard and I saw her collection when she lent it to the town library, where it commanded the glass case in the foyer reserved for rotating displays of citizens' treasures. We saw it again the next year, when it was displayed at Kelly's funeral.

But on the sunny spring afternoon that she and her mom first came to our door, Kelly felt she was the luckiest kid in the world. She was such an optimist that she often told her mom she was so lucky she had cancer and not cystic fibrosis or diabetes or Crohn's disease—she had met kids with these diseases and felt sorry for them, whereas what she had, she said, "really isn't so bad." But on this day she felt especially blessed—for she was about to meet a famous pig.

I had already put Chris out on his tether by the time Kelly

and Amy knocked at the door. With Tess and her Frisbee in tow, we approached the Plateau. Kelly couldn't believe her eyes.

"He's the biggest pig I've ever seen!"

"Want to pet him?" But I didn't really have to ask.

Over the next two years, Kelly and her mom were sporadic but enthusiastic visitors. Her parents had a photo of Chris enlarged to an eleven-by-fourteen-inch poster, which Kelly taped to her bedroom door. She told people it was "my friend Christopher, who lives up the road."

Kelly enjoyed telling her friends about her time with him. She would tell them how he would roll over so she could scratch his belly. "No!" they would say, disbelieving. *"Yeah!"* she would counter. She told them how he would leap to his hind legs when she visited him in the barn, and he would stand taller than she was, and hold open his mouth so she could plop in banana peels and apples and pastries. She told them about the feel of his bristles, and the special, gentle greeting grunt he gave her when she visited. They were always impressed.

But unlike Kate and Jane, Kelly never wanted to bring her friends to meet him. Her mom told me: "That was just for her and Christopher." The moments she spent with him were outside her everyday human friendships, and somehow seemed outside ordinary time. Kelly wore a knitted cap because her hair had fallen out; her cancer had spread to her spine and sometimes hurt terribly. But the cancer was far away when she came to visit Christopher Hogwood on the Pig Plateau. There was only a joyful, beaming young girl and the happiness of a great big pig.

. . .

"SO, WHAT DO YOU THINK?" I SAID TO KATE AND JANE ONE SUM-
mer afternoon at Pig Spa. I often consulted them on what I
was writing and they usually gave excellent advice. "Vampire
bats or sharks?"

As usual, I was working on several stories at a time. One,
for *Animals* magazine, had arisen from a recent jaunt with Liz
to Costa Rica, on which I'd enjoyed the distinction of being bitten by a vampire bat while I was removing the captured animal from a net. That story would report new findings that
these altruistic little creatures share blood meals with hungry
roost mates. The shark piece was for *International Wildlife,* the
story of Jaws in reverse: human hunger for shark-fin soup was
driving many sharks toward extinction. Which should I work
on first?

"Vampires," they said in unison.

"Unh," said Christopher, as if to register an opinion. He
moved a hind leg forward, asking us to scrub his butt.

It was one of those perfect, golden days on the cusp of September, when the late summer light spills over the land like
cricket song, and the fields are bright with goldenrod. The
hens bustled around us, hunting bugs and exclaiming softly;
Tess guarded us from her position at the edge of the tall grass.

We poured another cupful of warm rinse water over
Chris. "I might be a biologist when I grow up," Jane said.

"Really?"

"Or maybe an artist," she said. "Or maybe I would want to
travel and write." She paused. "Like you."

"When *I* grow up," Kate announced, "I'm going to start an
animal sanctuary." She had clearly given the idea quite a bit of
thought. "All the unwanted animals can come and stay with
me. It would be like here, like us with Chris and Tess and
everybody, but we would have elephants, too. And wolves.

And horses. And kids could come take care of them, kids who were runaways or homeless or having problems—"

"Unh-h-h-h-h-h!" said Christopher. The water was getting a tad too cool.

I could not help but think of Kelly then, forever fourteen. How grateful I was to have known her, and to keep her always in my memory. And how grateful I was for these girls with me now. I was grateful for their future, for the many bright dreams from which they would one day choose.

Like them, I, too, loved to imagine: my mind wandered the continents and paged through the unwritten books of tomorrow.

But that day, I was in no rush.

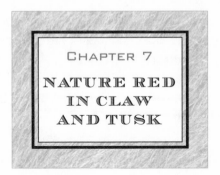

CHAPTER 7

NATURE RED IN CLAW AND TUSK

HOWARD WAS UPSTAIRS WITH HARRY ATWOOD, SOARING OVER Lake Erie in a flying boat in 1913. I was downstairs, gliding beneath the Pacific with hammerhead sharks over undersea mountains, sensing the earth's magnetic field as their guide.

But our written worlds vanished in an instant—casualties of another animal interruption. This time, it was the distress squawk of a chicken.

Not every squawk demanded our attention. Maybe somebody stole someone else's worm; a squabble erupted over nesting box space; a hen took offense at an undeserved peck. But sometimes squawks signaled another pig breakout. In an effort to steal the hens' grain, the coop was often the first stop on

Christopher's outings—the story of which we read clearly in his hoofprints in mud or snow.

Had Christopher escaped again? Only a couple of weeks earlier, Lilla and the girls had been getting ready for school when they saw him loose in their backyard, cheerfully flipping dinner-plate-sized divots of lawn into the air with his nose. Jane tried to lure him back to his pen with her peanut butter and jelly sandwich, but after he ate that, plus her apple, he took off down Route 137. His ultimate capture even involved our town road agent, so within days, the whole town had known our pig had been loose again.

We didn't want a replay of this soon.

Howard ran to look out the upstairs bathroom window, hoping not to see a black-and-white spotted pig crossing the street. Instead, he saw a hen racing uncharacteristically across the road.

Howard wondered: why did the chicken cross the road?

And then he saw, chasing the hen, something long and orange. Fox! The next moment, it had our hen in its jaws.

"Hey! Hey!" Howard called out the window. "Drop that chicken!"

The fox did.

Howard, Tess, and I rushed outside. We followed a Milky Way of downy feathers through the tall grass of our neighbor's field. At the end of it lay the hen, motionless, her tail gone. Howard bent down to pick up the corpse. At the sight of his shadow, she got up and ran away.

But where were the others? Eaten? Bleeding, frightened, hiding in the grass? We could only find four. We asked Tess for help. Whenever we found that a tenant's or a neighbor's cat had some poor chipmunk pinned to the lawn, all we had to do was say, "Tess—chase that cat!" Even though she wouldn't normally chase cats on her own, instantly she came to the rodent's rescue. But our brilliant Tess, normally so prescient about our desires, was oddly useless in this endeavor. She ran about barking, joyous at the unexpected outing. Chris probably knew what happened but had nothing to say.

We had heard about the fox at a party two weeks before. A vixen had dug her den in the soft dirt behind the town garage just down the street from us on Route 137. When the adorable kits emerged, the guys at the garage—most of them *Guns and Ammo* readers, guys who couldn't wait to shoot their deer each fall—began to offer the fox family food. As a result, the foxes grew so tame they hunted fearlessly in backyards in broad daylight.

They ate one of our neighbor's chickens, and then ate another neighbor's ducks. The girls held funerals for our hens. I suggested we start a Fox Victims Support Group on our street. We no longer let the Ladies out that spring unless we were there to guard them.

And then, one day, as Howard and I were working in the yard, with Christopher tethered on his Plateau and Tess at our side, the fox struck again. We chased him and shouted, but this time the orange bandit did not drop the bird. It bounded off into the woods with her in its black-lipped mouth. We never saw that hen again.

WE HAD BEEN THROUGH SUCH SORROWS BEFORE, AND WE WOULD endure them again. One spring night, someone dug through the dirt floor into our chicken coop, killed one of the hens, and, unable to drag the carcass back out through the small exit hole, left me to discover the carnage in the morning. The next night I set out a Havahart trap baited with chicken liver. By morning the culprit was in custody.

The caged skunk was regal and calm, with a composure

born of the confidence that a sac beneath its tail contained enough musk to clear the Pentagon. Skunks can spray up to twenty-three feet, and hit your face with accuracy at nine. Two nozzle-shaped nipples on either side of the anus can fire either an atomized spray or a stream of rain-sized droplets, as the skunk deems appropriate. Luckily, skunks aren't trigger-happy. I knew a New York researcher who tried to take a mouse away from a young skunk who was eating it; he was growled at, but not sprayed. Another researcher told me how he routinely picks up wild skunks *by their tails*.

Once I had explained this to Lilla, she let Jane miss the bus and accompany us on our mission to release the captured skunk. (Kate, alas, had already left for school.) With Howard at the wheel, as Jane and I spoke in low, soothing tones, the skunk rode uneventfully in the back of our Subaru to the grounds of the Harris Center. The captive waited patiently for me to open the trapdoor. Then it calmly stepped out, fluffed its magnificent tail, and waddled off into the forest with dignity, looking rather like a stout woman in a fur coat stepping out of a limousine. Jane was a celebrity at school for her role in the release.

The skunk never came back, but other predators did. Twice, neighbors' dogs attacked the flock. A hawk dove out of the sky and killed a hen instantly. Another time, it was a mink: we pieced together the predator's identity from the killing bite to the hen's throat and the tracks in the snow. The prints led to Moose Brook, where the mink had slipped beneath the ice and swum away.

We had considered a number of ways to protect our hens. Gretchen did not allow her chickens free range, but provided a spacious fenced outdoor pen. But sometimes a fence made things worse. One spring when Gretchen was raising broilers, she noticed a number of birds missing. There were no holes in the fence or tunnels dug beneath it. But a few telltale feathers stuck to the chicken wire fence told a gruesome tale: a visiting raccoon had grabbed birds one by one and pulled them out through the wire, essentially pureeing its prey.

We felt our hens were probably safer loose during the day, where, if they were attacked, their own considerable wits allowed them at least a chance of escape. At night, when most predators typically hunt, we always closed them in. One summer, though, two hens chose instead to roost each night atop Christopher Hogwood as he slept in his pen. Possibly they reasoned that few predators would dare bother them there. Or maybe they just liked his company.

Some evenings, when I would close the Ladies in, I would stay awhile and let their calm and sweetness wash over me. Howard caught me talking with them once: "Yes, you're my beauties," I whispered to them as they settled onto their night perches. I stroked their sleek backs and kissed their warm, rubbery combs. "I love you, Ladies."

But because we had chosen to live in this place—a place we loved because it was still partly wild—we accepted the bargain: nothing could guarantee their safety.

HUMAN RELATIONSHIPS WITH PREDATORS HAVE ALWAYS BEEN thorny. Predators are the first creatures our kind purposely eradicates. Too often, people feel humans are and should be in control; we are enraged to discover this is not true. And when other creatures share our appetites and kill our livestock (often animals we were raising to kill, ourselves), we call them vandals and murderers. Here in southern New England, town histories celebrate the wars waged against wolves, mountain lions, bobcats, bears. Our region's last wolf, a crippled female with three legs who had retreated to Mount Monadnock, was pursued for months by angry men from nearby towns. Wounded by gunfire, chased, and bludgeoned, she was finally shot to death in a hunt in the winter of 1820. Mountain lions, never numerous, were believed extinct in New Hampshire by 1850. Our black bears had disappeared by the century's end, although a bounty remained until 1957. Bobcats were nearly gone as well, though bounties persisted on them until 1972. Only in the last few decades, as our forests recover from a century of clear-cutting, unregulated hunting, and wasteful farming, are the predators returning to New Hampshire.

The story is the same around the world. Predators are the most persecuted creatures on Earth. If my life's work was, as I believed, to write about people's relationships with animals, it had been right to honor with my first book the three women scientists who changed forever our understanding of humankind's closest relatives. But next I was drawn to probe a more difficult relationship, one between people and predators—specifically tigers, the largest, most beautiful, and most deadly predators of all.

I planned to do my field research in a ten-thousand-square-kilometer mangrove swamp straddling India and Bangladesh along the Bay of Bengal, known as Sundarbans, which hosts the world's densest population of tigers. There is nowhere else like it on Earth. Here, for reasons no scientist understands, tigers routinely hunt people. They swim out into the ocean waves, swim after your boat like a dog chasing a car, climb on board, and eat you. In Sundarbans, tigers kill some three hundred people a year. And yet the people upon whom the tigers prey don't wish to eradicate the tigers. Instead, they worship them. I wanted to find out why.

. . .

"Tigers that *eat* people," Howard said, when I told him my book idea. He was not thrilled. "Oh, that's just great. Why can't you stay home and get eaten by your pig?"

(We did sometimes wonder whether Chris would eat us. We decided that, given the opportunity—if, for example, one of us suddenly dropped dead into his pen, and if he was hungry—he might. We didn't hold this against him. He would miss us afterward.)

My mother, too, voiced concern. In her weekly letters and in our phone conversations, she suggested that rather than visit "those mean ole tigers in that awful, *dirty* country," I instead "come on home" to Virginia—without Howard, of course—and write instead about the squirrels in the backyard. (My father had loved the squirrels and set out raisins and peanuts for them. My mother considered them edible rats. Growing up in Arkansas, she used to hunt and eat them.) I dismissed her worry as a mere social conceit: having a daughter eaten by a tiger might be a worse embarrassment to her than my having married a Jew.

Howard's misgivings, though, were quite real. But the thought that he worried something would happen to *me* didn't enter my mind. Surely he knew I was indestructible. What I thought irked him was the length, not the nature, of the field research. Researching *Spell of the Tiger,* I would be gone for months—leaving my husband to deal, alone, with hundreds of pounds of black and white problems.

When I was gone on day trips to Keene or to Boston, that's when Tess, normally so solicitous and refined, tended to roll in chicken droppings, poop in my office, or throw up on our bed. And what if something happened to the hens or the cockatiel while I was away? But, of course, the biggest source, quite literally, of potential disaster would be Christopher Hogwood.

Our pig was growing increasingly impressive, and not just in bulk. Once he turned two, his tusks were evident. At three, they were prominent. The lower tusks were short and sharp, and stuck out from the sides of his mouth. The upper tusks curled handsomely above his lip, like those of a warthog. I thought they lent him an even more cheerful, smiling aspect, though parents of young children who came to visit didn't always share this impression at first.

The Lillas and I admired Christopher's growing tusks. During Pig Spa, we were tempted to brush them. We decided against it. Looking back on it, this was probably wise.

It was the first Saturday in May, warm and sunny. The pig was out on his Plateau, rooting in the soft, wet earth, swishing away the first blackflies of spring with his wondrous tail. While Howard was out on an errand, I'd cleaned the house and finished the grocery shopping, and was looking forward to a visit from our friend Beth. It was the sort of day when you feel nothing can go wrong.

Howard and I had known Beth Bishop for a couple of years, but Tess had known her much longer. Beth worked as a volunteer at Evelyn's shelter. She was a serious animal lover, with a special spot in her heart for big, old dogs. Over the past fifteen years, Beth has adopted no fewer than eight huge, black Newfoundlands, many of them elderly. These lumbering, drooly Saint Bernard–sized beasts seemed incongruous roommates for Beth, a knockout platinum blonde whose makeup was always perfect. She was forty-six but looked twenty-six; on days she wore shorts, the checkout line to her cash register was always the longest at the A&P.

After her shift was over, nearly every day, Beth drove over to Evelyn's to help clean, walk, groom, and medicate the dozens of unwanted, injured, and rescued animals: A three-legged Great Pyrenees. A dachshund with a broken back. A cat injured in a steel-jaw leghold trap. A China white goose with a limp. A blind Pekingese. In Evelyn's log-cabin home, there was a room just for puppies down the hall from the bathroom, and a cattery downstairs. The horses grazed on the land across the street.

Beth remembered well the terrible day Tess had been injured, and the many months of her brave recovery. "Tess the Wonder Dog," Beth called her. She rejoiced when she learned that a local couple had adopted Tess; as it turned out, Beth lived just a mile from our house. When we finally met, Beth said, "Oh, you belong to Tess!" We'd been friends ever since.

With her soft spot for huge beasts, naturally Beth adored Christopher—she considered him "the Newfie of pigdom"—and when she came to visit, she always brought him treats: bruised melons, wilting lettuce, expired bread the A&P was throwing away. And that was the case on this day. We had just poured out a slops feast for him and stepped back to watch him eat.

But then Beth reached toward Chris, as if he were in fact a Newfie, to give him a pat on the head. He might have thought she wanted to take her garbage back—which she did not—for he nudged her out of the way with the side of his head. It was nothing aggressive. He didn't bark or growl. He didn't even give her a dirty look (pigs' eyes are very expressive—one of our friends claimed Christopher had eyes like the actor Claude Rains, who played the cynical police chief in *Casablanca*). Beth said nothing, but I noticed a red slice on the inside of her left thigh, about seven inches below the hem of her shorts—a slice so deep that it revealed the yellow layer of subcutaneous fat above the muscle.

Christopher had caught her with the edge of one lower

tusk. The tooth was so sharp she hadn't felt the cut. Neither one of them had any idea what had happened.

But now the wound was dripping blood.

"Uh, Beth," I said, trying to sound very, very calm, "I think Chris might have clipped you with his tusk just now."

She glanced at her leg. Because of the location of the injury, she couldn't really see how bad it was. "Oh, it'll be OK," she said. She was used to 150-pound Newfies leaping up on her and raking her accidentally with their claws. "Do you think I need a Band-Aid?"

It was going to need more than a Band-Aid.

"I think the cut might be kind of deep," I mentioned casually. "In fact, it might be a good idea to drop by the hospital, just to let them take a look."

Now Beth was worried. "I don't want a shot," she said. "I hate shots! And I'm not going to do stitches. Promise me they won't do stitches."

The emergency room physician took one look at the wound, pulled out an immense needle, gave Beth an injection that hurt much worse than the injury, and put in four stitches. In the small box on the medical form where you describe the event that prompted the visit to the emergency room, the doctor wrote "pig collision."

When Beth went home that evening, she had a hankering for music. She turned on the stereo and put on the album of her choice: Fleetwood Mac's *Tusk*.

THOUGH I WAS APPALLED AT THE ACCIDENT, BETH WAS NEVER THE least bit angry. The next day, though Beth missed work (we insisted on paying her lost wages), she still limped over to our house to see Chris again. As always, Chris and Beth were delighted to see each other. Nothing between them had changed.

"I didn't have to go to therapy for pig-phobia or anything," Beth said. "To me, it wasn't a negative thing at all," she insisted. "It added some excitement to my life!"

The next day, when she did return to work, she wore shorts again, revealing a huge bandage. Hers was not just the longest but also the slowest lane at the checkout counter that day. Everyone wanted to hear the story. "Christopher didn't attack me," she explained to each customer. "It was a mistake. His tusks stuck out. He couldn't help it."

To make matters worse, Beth's wound became infected. She had to make several follow-up visits to the hospital. The medical paperwork reflected mounting concern. The "event" box for the second visit did not read "pig collision" but was changed to "pig bite." By her final visit, the event had had escalated to "gored by pig."

It was clear that something had to be done about Christopher's tusks, and fast.

Chris didn't mean to hurt anyone. He was a gentle soul. He was famously patient with children, particularly with kids who were shy—his grunts were softer and his movements slower, something that sensitive parents always noted with amazement. Chris was fine around people in wheelchairs, too, which not all animals are; some dogs, for instance, chase and bite wheelchairs the same way others chase cyclists. A big pig such as Chris could easily upend a wheelchair or puncture its tires. And this was a concern when Liz's daughter, Stephanie, a disability rights activist who has used a wheelchair since a teenage spinal injury, first came to see Chris on a holiday visit with her husband, Bob. Bob is a fellow activist who uses a chair, too. The first time they came, they watched from their van as we let Chris run past the windshield like some warthog at a safari park. But later (with Stephie's strong brother, Ramsay, a mountain guide, standing by in case of the need for a quick retreat) everyone met *en plein air.* Chris sniffed the tires on the wheelchairs with curiosity but didn't try to bite them. He and Stephie and Bob got on famously, and we knew we could count on him to be polite with later visitors in wheelchairs, too.

But still—without realizing the danger of his own tusks, what if Christopher literally ran into someone on one of his jaunts around town? What if a child was injured?

All twenty or so species of wild pigs, both males and females, grow tusks and know well how to use them—usually with admirable restraint. The extravagant upper tusks are not particularly dangerous. Warthogs and babirusas employ them for largely symbolic head-to-head clashes, from which the loser escapes by kneeling and squealing; the victor turns and walks away. Most pigs, in fact, resolve their conflicts peacefully. Peccaries, for instance, often squabble but seldom really fight. Invariably, quarreling peccaries end up at some point nose to rump, a position that allows them to imbibe the elixir of these pigs' most potent scent glands, located at the rear. At this point, the contestants are apparently overwhelmed by the intoxicating delights of each other's piggy perfume and their anger is defused. Upon inhaling the essence of the rival, "both stop struggling," reports biologist Lyall Watson, who has seen this in the wild. In his fine book on pigs of the world, *The Whole Hog,* he describes how "their eyes half close, and a soft, dreamy look steals over their faces." All is forgiven.

Wild boars, too, usually manage to avoid bloodshed. They will stand shoulder to shoulder and lean against each other and try to throw the other down by wedging a snout under the rival's hip, whereupon the dispute is usually considered settled.

But the wild card in predicting the outcome of porcine aggression is this: pigs are extremely emotional. They can be deeply devoted and intuitive. But like people, they are also prone to sulks, irrational fears, and tantrums. The behaviorist Ivan Pavlov once worked with pigs but gave up on them. "All pigs," he concluded, "are hysterical."

With their tusks and great bulk, their omnivorous diet and sometimes frightening voices, it is easy to forget that pigs are ungulates. But hooves don't lie. Hooves are the heritage of flight: eons of running away sculpted the hardened tiptoes that define the ungulates, from antelopes to horses, from goats to pigs to giraffes. Deep in their genes, pigs remember. Forty million years of porcine evolution says: somebody is trying to eat you. Forty thousand years of barnyard history says: somebody *is* going to eat you. Who wouldn't be hysterical?

Howard and I simply could not afford to be responsible for an hysterical 350-pound pig blunderbussing through Hancock armed with razor-sharp tusks. For the good of the community, we had but one choice: tuskectomy.

I knew Chris wasn't going to like it, but I phoned Tom Dowling. Tom was a vet with a practice in a neighboring town. He had earned his master's degree in pigs. We had first become acquainted the year before, due to a math error. As part of routine hog husbandry, Howard and I wormed Christopher annually. That year, I had gone to buy the medicine at Agway. When you buy it in bulk, the drug is packaged for a lot of little pigs, not one big pig. I calculated the dose wrong. Hours after he had swallowed the medicine, Christopher came down with what looked like a terrible stomachache. I had poisoned him!

Who in the area treated pigs? George and Mary's pig vet was too far away. We had a wonderful vet for Tess, but at the time I did not know he treated large animals, too. Based on a horse-owning friend's recommendation, I summoned Tom. At the sight of the tall, lanky vet entering his pen, Chris struggled to his feet, trying to greet his visitor. Expertly, Tom got a loop of rope over Christopher's snout, and to my amazement, Chris's reaction—a known reflex among pigs—was to stand as if frozen in his tracks, screaming but eerily unable to move, enabling Tom to squirt liquid-activated charcoal down Christopher's throat to neutralize the excess wormer.

Although Chris didn't thrash, he still managed to dramatically register his displeasure. A pig's screams can be quite literally deafening, a health threat deemed serious enough to merit an article in the *Journal of the American Veterinary Medical Association* titled "Incidence of Hearing Loss in Swine Veterinarians." *"Ree! Ree! Ree-e-e-e-e!"* Christopher shrieked, at the same time shooting thick streams of liquid charcoal out of his nose and mouth. When the eruption was over, Tom was as black as a chimney sweep. But Christopher was all right.

So it was to Tom I turned again. Because Christopher had met Tom only once, well over a year before, I hoped he wouldn't remember him. But unfortunately, Christopher seemed to have excellent recall. He never forgot the location of the Amidon lettuce garden, for instance, and it was clear Christopher remembered a number of people and recognized them easily. (I later learned this is typical of pigs: laboratory tests show pigs easily outperform dogs in learning mazes, and pigs can recognize people not only by smell but also by sight alone. Pigs can also discriminate between people at a distance, even when the people are wearing identical clothes.) That Christopher remembered people was obvious in his greeting grunts. His grunts were low and soft for Kate and Jane, deep and manly for Howard; there was one distinctive grunt he used only for our friend Ray Cote. The president of a software company, Ray's busy schedule permitted only rare visits. But each time he came to his pen, Chris emitted deep, loud, long, fantastically appreciative greetings he offered no other person. Why? Ray and Chris had much in common: they were both smart and strong and funny. But what Chris may have liked best was that Ray weighed about four hundred pounds. Chris may have thought he had finally found one of His People.

But would our pig remember Tom? The minute Hogwood caught sight of him, he began to shriek hysterically—and didn't stop until Tom had finished sawing (painlessly, he promised) both of Christopher's sharp lower tusks to blunt, harmless stubs.

YOU MIGHT THINK I'D HAVE BEEN AS WORRIED ABOUT THE JAWS OF Sundarbans's tigers as I was about the tusks of our pig. I was not. Truth be told, my getting eaten was never one of my worries. My worries about the trip were all centered on Hancock, that something bad might happen while I was gone. I never would have admitted it, but the hardest part of any trip I ever took was leaving home.

I was vulnerable to homesickness—but immune, in my mind, to death. I could not even fathom my husband's and my mother's concern for me. I was too lucky to die, but I reckoned that even if I did, getting eaten was a fine way for me to go. Plus, if I got nailed by an experienced tiger, it probably wouldn't hurt. Tigers stalk and ambush hunters, and almost always attack from the back. A skilled tiger sinks its canines into the spaces between the neck vertebrae of its prey, severing the spinal cord as neatly as a key opens a lock. In Sundarbans, it's said that people attacked by tigers are often killed so quickly they don't have time to scream.

I almost got a chance to find out. On my first expedition, my boat got stuck in the mud in an area where tigers were known to be hiding. My boatman, Girindra Nath Mridha, handed me a machete and my photographer an ax. During the endless minutes that Girindra and his son worked to push the craft free, we stood back to back on the deck of the boat with only these weapons to defend our party against the tiger if it chose to attack.

Later, we had an even closer call. We chugged down a wide river and then turned up a small channel. Fearful of getting stuck, Girindra turned the boat around—to reveal tiger tracks so fresh that they couldn't have been more than two minutes old. But the tiger had not simply swum across the little channel; there were no prints on the opposite bank. We backtracked to the larger river and, to our amazement, discovered that the tiger had entered the water from the forest there. The tiger had swum after our boat.

Through it all, Girindra, a strong, slight man my age who had seen an uncle killed by a tiger, was never angry. He feared the tiger, but he did not hate it. Like his fellow villagers, Girindra would never hurt a tiger except in direct self-defense. No one poached tigers in Sundarbans. To search out a tiger to kill it was unthinkable.

What, I wondered, did they know about predators that most people have forgotten?

To research the book, I went back to Sundarbans again and again. At first I stayed at the little tourist lodge across the river from Girindra's village. But later, with a translator, I stayed with Girindra's family—his beautiful wife, Namita, his mother, MaBisaka, and his eight children—at the smooth mud and thatch house they had made by hand. They were eager to help with my book. By day, in Girindra's wooden boat, we would search the banks of the muddy creeks for tiger signs. At night, the neighbors—fishermen, honey gatherers, widows— would gather at his home, smoking clove-scented bidis and chewing betel nut, and by the light of the kerosene lamp they would tell me stories of tigers and crocodiles, gods and ghosts. After they would go, I would lie in the darkness, trying not to think of Christopher's ears or Howard's laugh, or the way that

Tess would now lie on her back on our bed and expose her white belly to us in complete, trusting bliss. Home seemed as far away as a half-remembered dream, and the thought of it would seize my throat with a sob.

When I came home, it was Sundarbans that felt like a dream. Which was the dream and which was real? Girindra's letters reminded me: both were real. We wrote each other regularly—we still do—my letters translated into Bengali and his to me into English by the teacher at the village school. "*Amar chotto bon,*" his letters usually begin, "my little sister." Shortly after my second trip to Sundarbans, Girindra, who as a Hindu believes in multiple lifetimes, announced that he thought he and I had been brother and sister in a former life. Girindra's eight children called me *pishima,* the beautiful Bengali word for paternal aunt.

"Take atop my love," Girindra would write. "I pray you are well by the blessings of Goddess." I prayed even harder for him and his family; after all, they lived on the outskirts of a reserve inhabited by five hundred man-eating tigers. "Thank you very much to write long treasurous letter. I used to wait for the same as a thirsty bird and inquire to the postal department...." I did, too. Pat knew well how eagerly I awaited Girindra's letters. We wrote each other about every two weeks, but it usually took a month for a letter to arrive, sometimes more.

Each battered airmail letter, covered with as many as fourteen stamps, was blessed proof the family had survived. In grateful reply I composed simple but detailed letters describing life in our village on the other side of the world. I sent photos: our post office and church in five feet of new snow; a picture of my father in his military uniform; Howard and me in parkas and snowshoes. I sent pictures of Kate and Jane and Lilla, Ed and Pat. And, of course, I often sent pictures of our animals. ("Your very large Hogwood pig is wonder to see,"

Girindra wrote. "There is no such pig in Sundarbans. How can it be? It is as miracle to us.")

But the miracle, to me, was in Girindra's world, where death in the jaws of a predator was a subject as familiar as the weather. "Rain has fled along with its wetty clumsyness," he wrote in one letter; in the next paragraph: "A large grown-up crocodile has been a terror to the fishing persons. Five man and woman have been eaten within a month and a half." Yet in Sundarbans, there would never be a posse of hunters tracking down a croc or a tiger, even a man-eater, the way New Hampshire's early farmers had persecuted Monadnock's last, crippled wolf. That was the central mystery in my book, the mystery that kept me returning to Sundarbans.

I learned the answer from the story of the tiger god. The story is retold in Sundarbans each January in a long poetic song, part of a day of praise and propitiation to Daskin Ray, ruler of Sundarbans. He is at once a tiger and a god. The crocodiles and sharks are his emissaries. Daskin Ray has always owned the riches of Sundarbans—the fishes, the trees, the bees and their honey—and it is only through his generosity that he shares these gifts with the people. But only if the people understand that the forest is his, and give both him and the land due respect. To this day, they say, the deity may still enter the body of a tiger at any moment, and if the god has been angered, he will attack.

The stories reflect a sophisticated understanding of ecology. The tiger protects the forest: fear of the tiger keeps woodsmen from cutting down all the mangroves. The mangroves protect the coastline: their limbs and leaves soften the winds of cyclones. Their roots form nurseries for fish, which feed the people. The people understand that without the tiger, Sundarbans could not stay whole.

That a man may be eaten by a tiger does not make life

cheap. No; in Sundarbans, life is large, and gods are every-where for the people to see. So the people see the tiger's mission in life—its dharma—as sacred. They see the holy goddess who resides in every cow. They remember that the great god Vishnu once came to Earth as a boar. And they see, as well, in the jaws of the tiger, the blameless perfection of the divine.

In one of his books, Howard writes about a concept called *tikkun:* it's a term coined by a Kabbalist mystic, and proceeds from an ancient Jewish story about the beginning of the world. The story has it that shortly after Creation, some of the Lord's light, the creative force, was spilled and lost by accident. It is our job, says the mystic, to try, in our actions, to gather up that spilled light—to restore the wholeness of the world.

But what is wholeness? How do we come to recognize it, and to realize when it is lost?

I know how wholeness feels. It feels like the soft summer evenings when I would close in Christopher and the chickens for the night. It feels like when Tess would lie on our bed and roll on her back to show us her white belly. It feels like the times I would linger by the barn as soft clucks and gentle grunts would wash over me like moonlight, and fill me with peace.

Wholeness feels like gratitude. Gratitude that we are safe and happy and together. And for that, I must thank equally the foxes and the weasels, the tigers and the crocodiles. For the peace of the barnyard, I am grateful to the dangers and jaws of the jungle. For the belonging that is home, I can thank, in part, the exile that is travel. Though they seem like opposites, they are more like twins—two halves of a whole.

CHAPTER 8
CELEBRITY

THE PHOTOGRAPHER HAD DRIVEN UP FROM NEW YORK. HIS CRE-
dentials were impressive: he used to work for Time-Life.
Bruce Curtis had covered the war in Vietnam, where he had
been wounded three times. He had documented the student
protests at home, the Yom Kippur War in the Middle East, the
famine in Biafra.

And now, with a car trunk full of camera equipment and
costume props, here he was on our doorstep. Again, he was
shooting on location.

His next stop was the Pig Plateau.

Bruce had heard about Christopher from his girlfriend,
who had met Howard years before on a Victorian Society

study program in England. Bruce had quit Time-Life and now worked freelance, hustling after any image that would sell: teddy bears wearing different outfits, bucolic landscapes. He thought a big spotted pig would make a great subject for a series of greeting cards.

The props reflected those he had in mind. For a birthday card, he envisioned the pig wearing a party hat, surrounded by festively wrapped packages with bows, and in the foreground, a birthday cake. For a new-baby card, he had made up signs that said IT'S A BOY! and IT'S A GIRL! and procured various pink and blue items for Christopher to wear to celebrate the appropriate sex. Then there was a wild and crazy party invitation idea, with an assortment of hats and some giant, hot-pink plastic sunglasses, the kind you get at an amusement park. Another theme would be the pig in a bubble bath, with all sorts of soaps and shampoos and a shower cap.

Howard and I welcomed him to New Hampshire. After all, he was a friend of Howard's friend. Besides, how could I refuse someone who considered our pig such a worthy portrait subject?

Howard didn't say so, but he did not think Chris would cooperate. My husband retreated to his upstairs office to write. Kate and Jane were off on some neighborhood adventure. I was left alone to work as Bruce's pig wrangler.

Bruce was initially enthusiastic. We had a beautiful July day. The light was clear and rich. Our barn was "the perfect color." But when Bruce actually met Christopher, whom I had already put out on his tether, the photographer was taken aback.

"He's much bigger than I expected," he said soberly.

"He's much bigger than we expected, too," I replied.

Bruce studied the scene with his photographer's eye. "What's that nylon webbing around him for?" He was concerned that the makeshift harness, patched as it was with pieces of different-colored nylon from previous generations, would look bad in the photos.

"That's the only thing between us and four hundred pounds of loose pig," I explained.

"You mean you *can't control him?*"

"Not at all," I answered honestly. "He's pretty much the one in control around here."

When he'd envisioned his project, Bruce might have hoped that Christopher would turn out to be a porcine version of one of William Wegman's vogueish weimaraners. But this was not to be.

Christopher hated the party hats. The flimsy elastic, made to stretch around the chin of a child's seven-pound head, instantly snapped when we tried to stretch it around Christopher's hundred-pound head and the commodious jowls that hung from it. We tried to perch the hats between his ears, but they tickled. If Kate had been on hand—her wardrobe genius now perfected in the fashion crucible of junior high—maybe she could have gotten him to wear them, but without her it was hopeless. Christopher shook each hat off in turn, and when it fell to the ground, he would pick it up in his mouth and deliver the death shake. We had a party pack of twelve shiny, pointy hats. Within five minutes, he had destroyed eleven of them.

We obviously needed to get a hat on him before we set out the birthday cake, which would last perhaps two seconds, if that, before Chris ate it. But perhaps we should try piling the gifts first, then the hat, and finally the cake, I suggested. Christopher knocked the boxes over instantly with his nose. He had pioneered the knocking-things-over game with our carefully stacked woodpile, but this was even more fun, because the next step, as he saw it, was obviously to rip off the gift wrap. He pinned each box with a hoof and then tore off the wrapping with his lips, giving this a shake, too, before shredding it.

Finally we decided to nix the gifts and just focus on the hat and the cake. Once the cake was served, we would have just one chance for the shot. Bruce set his camera on its tripod just out of nose-print range. I set a few bagels on the ground to occupy Chris while I got the final hat and the cake. I plunked the hat on the pig, set down the cake, and darted away from the camera. The hat fell off. Christopher plowed his nose through the blue HAPPY on the white icing, and then, in one bite, consumed one-quarter of the sheet cake.

Christopher was enjoying his modeling career immensely. The only parts he didn't like were wearing clothes and getting photographed.

For the new-baby card, Christopher shook off every piece of pink and blue ornament Bruce had to offer. He would not put his front legs through the sleeves of a sweater—and besides, it was the wrong size anyway. He pushed over, pulled up, shook and bit the IT'S A BOY! and IT'S A GIRL! signs until they were pulp.

The only thing Hogwood consented to wear was a red kerchief around his neck, which Bruce put on to cover the unsightly harness. That, and—oddly—the giant sunglasses. He liked them. They perched comfortably on his wide snout, and the colored lenses ended up positioned, uncannily, directly in front of his eyes. He walked around with the glasses on his face for about a minute. Bruce got several shots before they slid off Chris's head.

Finally—the props broken, the cake eaten, the wardrobe destroyed—Bruce and I made the final effort, the bubble bath scene. The harness would have to come off, Bruce said; Chris had to be naked for the bath. We frothed up some bubbles in a bucket of warm water and I unbuckled the harness.

But Christopher Hogwood had had enough. He took off at a trot to a neighbor's house, where he could smell their wild grapes ripening.

BRUCE'S HARD DAY'S WORK, WE FEARED, HAD BEEN A BUST. BUT this was not true. The shot of Hogwood wearing the giant glasses came out beautifully. Bruce generously sent us a copy with his permission to use this however we liked. It gave us an idea.

For years, we had received holiday greetings from our smiling friends in their gracious homes, photos of their chubby-cheeked infants, and newsletters detailing the academic and sporting achievements of their successful children. A writer for the *New York Times* style section once called the annual family Christmas card "a billboard of wealth, position, marital status and procreative success." Now we could join that tradition. Except we were unemployed, childless freelance writers. It was obvious what we should do: send out holiday photos of our pig.

We figured we owed as much to our friends. For Christopher was, in a sense, a community effort. By now, Christopher commanded a vast slops empire. Besides the girls next door, the postmistress, and the minister, regular contributors included the world's top experts on wildebeests. Lovers of all hoofed creatures, Dr. Richard Estes, a biologist who has spent half a century flying between New Hampshire and Tanzania studying antelopes, and his wife, Runi, whom he had married during a break in the wildebeest rut, saved their kitchen garbage for Chris all week, keeping it in bags in their freezer. I picked it up at their house on Saturdays (and more than once brought home a bag of frozen shrimp or a whole frozen chicken by mistake). Cindy Dechert, who lived across from her parents, the Amidons, brought Christopher an old-fashioned leafy forage called mangles, cut fresh from her garden. Barry Estabrook, the editor of my first published collection of *Boston Globe* columns, mailed Chris stale bread from the bakery across the street from his office in northern Vermont. In late summer, Hogwood's bowl overflowed with Hancock's surplus zucchini; at first frost, gardeners brought him green tomatoes caught on the vine; after Halloween, the wheelbarrow in the upstairs barn was heaped high with donated pumpkins.

And all this on top of perhaps the most impressive slops score of Christopher's career: the Wide World Cheese Shop. Although Howard and I could rarely afford to eat out, our pig now enjoyed a regular supply of gourmet foods from one of the most popular luncheon spots in the area, a seven-mile drive away, over in the next town.

Red leaf lettuce. Sourdough bread. Dill Havarti cheese. The first and last slices of the tomato. And soups—lots of soups. "If it burned," the cheese shop's chef and owner, Harlow Richardson, told us, "the soup went Cajun. But if it went beyond that, it went to Christopher." All these delicacies went into the green, five-gallon pickle pails stationed beneath the prep counter, and from there into Harlow's Chevy pickup. In a rural area where even pizza delivery was unheard of, Christopher Hogwood alone received regular door-to-stall deliveries. Harlow even served Christopher music with his meal. Harlow usually showed up singing—*The Pirates of Penzance, The Mikado, Orpheus in the Underworld,* whatever community performance for which he was currently rehearsing—and Christopher quickly grew to love opera.

We owed many others in town for their escort services. How many times had Ed rescued Christopher? How often had Mike herded him off the dangerous state road? Then there was the time we had driven to Long Island for Thanksgiving and returned to the scene of every homeowner's worst nightmare: the entire volunteer fire department was at our house. We saw no fire truck, but we recognized everyone's car. As it turned out, Chris had escaped and everyone had shown up to make sure he got back to the barn safely.

We initially sent out a hundred Christopher cards. Then we started getting requests from people who hadn't gotten one. We had to go back to the camera shop and ask them to print more.

BRUCE DIDN'T REALIZE IT, BUT HE WAS FOLLOWING IN A GRAND tradition. The oldest known picture of a pig is the image of a leaping boar painted forty thousand years ago in the cave of Altamira in northern Spain. Artists have drawn fresh inspiration from pigs ever since. One source, the artist-author of *The Pig in Art,* even suggests that the most famous early image of a woman—the zaftig limestone figurine known as "Venus of Willendorf," dated between 24,000 to 22,000 B.C.—might really be an indirect homage to a pig. (The idea is less outlandish than it sounds, considering that pigs have long been seen as symbols of fecundity. And no one would deny that this Venus looks pretty porky.)

The first domestic pigs depicted in human art seem to be Chinese offerings found in Zhou tombs dated to the ninth century B.C. Since then, as pigs have continued to inspire us with their bravery and fecundity, as they have fed both our bodies and our spirits, it's no wonder humans have celebrated pigs in almost every imaginable medium: Chinese pigs of jade, Egyptian swine of ebony. Pigs carved from rhino horn and elephant ivory. Pigs in terra cotta and porcelain. The Vatican houses a life-sized marble sculpture of a great white mother pig, and the Louvre enshrines a frieze of an Assyrian sow and her piglets among its art treasures.

When we sent out those first pig Christmas cards when Chris was only five, we had no grandiose plans. But Chris had been born beneath a lucky star. He had what every great soul needs to make his mark in the world: gravitas. (At five hundred pounds and counting, that is true gravitas.) Fame, of a sort, found him.

Letter addressed to Christopher Hogwood, from Blanchard & Blanchard Ltd. of Norwich, Vermont, manufacturer of "pure and fancy foods from Vermont":

Dear Mr. Hogwood,
We know you appreciate fine gourmet foods . . .

Tess, too, had been the recipient of bulk mail sent to our address (One read: "As CEO of your company, you . . .") But this one was unnerving. *How did they know?*

From the police log of the *Monadnock Ledger:*

HANCOCK—Fame was too much for Christopher the pig, who appeared on the Boston television show *Chronicle* on Thursday. The day after his appearance Christopher escaped from his home. Police responded to Old Antrim Road and looked for him, but could not find him. His owner, Sy Montgomery, found him later. Said Chief Ed Coughlan, "He can't take the publicity."

From the *Peterborough Transcript:*

A photo op with Christopher Hogwood, a huge pig owned by Sy Montgomery and Howard Mansfield of Hancock, was one of the prizes auctioned off at a fund-raiser for Peterborough's cultural museum, the Mariposa Museum. The highest bidder—Jim Jenkins of Antrim—was named Hog Reeve for Life.

From election news in the *Keene Sentinel:*

HANCOCK—No one filed for election as town moderator and Thomas Ward won with 69 write-in votes. He easily beat Selectman Neal Cass and Christopher Hogwood, who each got three write-in votes. Hogwood is a pig owned by Howard Mansfield and Sy Montgomery. Voters apparently want an exciting town meeting next year; their new moderator isn't a boar.

Howard sometimes accused me of being a stage mother. This wasn't really true. Yes, if the local press needed a photo when I had a new book coming out, I always wanted Chris in the picture. I was proud of our pig. But I was also shrewd enough to realize that the wrong camera angle can make even a size four look fat—but not if I'm standing beside an enormous hog.

Our photos together appeared in the local weeklies. We were in the big-city daily, the *Keene Sentinel.* (The *Sentinel* reporter's first question to me was about Chris, and, I thought, rather personal. "Does he fart?" he asked. "Rarely," I demurred.) We were also on TV together. The editor who had mailed Christopher bread from a Vermont bakery had published a second collection of my columns, among which was an essay on mud—New Hampshire's most abundant natural re-source during the month of March, and the subject of a segment on the Boston TV show *Chronicle*. But Christopher, as always, stole the show. He was, after all, a bigger expert on mud than I. The cameraman wisely devoted much footage to letting Hogwood demonstrate the highest and best use of this splendid substance. He pushed it around with his nose, looked at the camera, pronounced "Unh!" (as if to say, "Like so"), and rolled over. George happened to be over at Gretchen's house, shoeing one of her ponies, when the program aired. "George, you won't believe it!" Gretchen cried, "Christopher Hogwood is on TV!" George raced inside to watch. All through the segment, George was silent, shaking his head in amazement. Finally he spoke. "That pig," George said to Gretchen, "has done awfully well for himself."

Chris's photo appeared in the *Boston Globe*. It had nothing to do with my column. It was a stand-alone photo in the state section of the New Hampshire edition. I knew the photographer, because he specialized in wildlife and because he and his wife ran a rehabilitation center for injured owls in Massachusetts. He stopped by our barn to say hello one day when he was in the area. Next thing we knew, Hogwood occupied a quarter page of the Sunday newspaper. He was standing on his hind legs with his forelegs resting on the gate, foaming drool cascading from his jaws, anticipating a bagel. "Animals are favorite photo subjects and pigs can be very photogenic," read the caption, "but Pavlov's hog, a.k.a. Christopher Hogwood, stretches things as he comes drooling toward the camera in search of dinner." (I thought indignantly that the caption writer was too gauche to appreciate Christopher's fashion statement: a pig accessorizes with drool.)

His photo also appeared in the *Washington Post,* where Howard's best friend from college and his wife worked as reporters. (Their kids had done Pig Spa and loved it.) For several years after *The Hidden Life of Dogs* became a bestseller, Liz Thomas wrote a column for *USA Today*—and managed to work in a reference to Christopher Hogwood there. He was mentioned frequently on New Hampshire Public Radio. "That was Hayden's Symphony No. 84 in E-flat Major," the classical music program's host would announce, "Christopher Hogwood conducting." Occasionally he would also reference our barnyard opera-lover. Even when he did not, we got comments from our neighbors: "Heard your pig on the radio today."

But Hogwood's most wide-reaching media coverage resulted from Howard's literary efforts. *Yankee* magazine often published Howard's articles on historic preservation and New England icons. Christopher became one of the latter. The editors titled Howard's article about Chris "It's a Hog's Life." The subtitle asked: "Food, Visitors and Media Attention—What More Could a Pig Want?"

"Our pig is a Zen eater," Howard explained. "He becomes his food. He is his food. He loves his food. No remorse. No guilty dinner chat about fat or sugar or pesticides. A pig brings us back to a simpler time in our dining history: all food is good food."

No wonder, my husband wrote, that so many people bring him slops. "It's as if the whole world tilts and vegetables roll toward the commodious jaws of our pig. . . .

"Over the past five years, " Howard boasted, "Christopher Hogwood has built a larger constituency than most congressmen. . . . For someone who spends most of his time in his pen or outside sunning himself, he sure can network."

As a result of Howard's story, the network only expanded. One day as we were leaving to visit friends for supper, a car with California plates pulled up in front of the house. "Does

Christopher Hogwood live here?" the driver, a middle-aged fellow, asked. "My wife and I read about him in *Yankee*. We wondered if we could take a picture."

We escorted the West Coast paparazzi to Christopher's stall. When we drove off, they were still taking photos.

AS CHRISTOPHER'S NETWORK AND GIRTH EXPANDED, SO DID OUR mailing list. More and more people wanted Chris's picture: the editors at all the papers, magazines, and publishers for which we wrote, Howard's associates in historic preservation, story sources at universities and museums. Most of them had heard a parrot squawk or a dog bark during telephone calls to us, and since I had taken to augmenting our chicken flock every second or third spring by raising baby chicks under a heat lamp in my office, often folks would hear chicks peeping as well. "Are you calling from a zoo?" they would wonder. Not exactly . . . but we would end up telling them about our animal family, and Christopher. We would send a card. They loved seeing a happy pig wearing pink sunglasses. They all wanted to know when the next card was coming out.

Christopher's holiday cards became a tradition, another way of marking time. There was the year Christopher wore the elf hat. Then there was the year we featured Chris drinking a Schlitz. (Some of our friends accused us of pig abuse. We weren't sure whether they thought alcohol wasn't good for pigs, or whether they simply didn't like Schlitz.)

One year, Jane's birthday fell during the Perseid meteor showers, and we all lay out in the backyard counting shooting stars. Between meteors, we wondered: what should we do for next year's pig photo? How can we top last year's?

But that was the summer Lilla told us that she and the girls would be moving away. The divorce and its aftermath had cleaned Lilla out. As a single mother with two kids to support, Lilla now turned to her own mother for help. But she lived in Connecticut. The family would have to move there.

The day before the move, we held an all-day Pig Spa. Lilla was next door packing. Howard was upstairs in his office, trying to write, feeling empty and sad. Kate and Jane and I were down at the Plateau, brushing Christopher in the sun. Kate looked up. "I want to do Pig Spa again tomorrow!" she said.

We reminded each other that Connecticut was not so far away. We would visit. The girls would come back to Hancock for a couple of weeks every summer.

But there would be no Pig Spa tomorrow. The sweet old house next door would be empty. It seemed too awful to bear. The three of us flung our arms around each other and over the pig's prone body. As he grunted softly, we sobbed into his bristles.

CHAPTER 9

FINDING EDEN

"There's Jane's bus." Every morning, as I served the eggs our hens had given, Howard would sit at the wobbly card table by the window and make this wistful observation as the elementary school bus went by. But Jane, of course, was not on it.

The Doll House stood empty. The sweet little cape now looked sad to us, as if it were as lonely for its former occupants as we were.

We missed the girls terribly, and we worried over who would move in next door. What if they had aggressive dogs who ran loose, or kids who chased or teased animals? Would our hens be safe? What if they didn't like our pig? Christopher's hefty manure heap was composting just inches from the stone wall that separated our two yards. What if the new people didn't like pig manure?

We had a long wait to find out. Though the owner of the house moved back in for a while, he lost his job as a buyer for a sporting goods company, and soon the bank foreclosed on the house. New Hampshire had hit another recession, and this time the real estate market, too, was slow. But in this case, the real estate agent had an additional challenge—one we didn't know about until Christopher's special friend, the software expert, Ray Cote, told us about a conversation he'd had with the agent at a Chamber of Commerce gathering.

"We had this couple up from New Jersey," the agent told Ray. "They were looking for a nice, quiet place, sort of out of the way, so I showed them this house. We did the entire inside of the house and they liked it. They were very happy with it. We went outside and there was this beautiful garden back there, with flowers in bloom, and they were really enjoying it. They were *really* looking like they were interested in the house. I thought they were going to make an offer. The husband was just about to say something to me—at which point we heard this yell.

"And I looked over to this other yard, next door. And there is this little, skinny, five-foot-five woman, wearing these huge floppy boots, and she is running as fast as she absolutely could. And she is carrying this bucket, which is obviously heavy, and running like mad. Why on earth is she running?

"So we look behind her. And what we saw was this: The head of an enormous black and white hog. And then we saw the body of an enormous hog. And then some more of the body of this hog. This hog is thundering out of nowhere. And it's running after her making loud, snorting noises. Snort, snort, snort! *Snort, snort, snort!* And then the woman goes *flying* into the barn. And the pig goes *flying* into the barn. And then the door slams. And then there's silence."

"So what did you say to the couple?" Ray asked.

"I turned to them and said, 'So it's a nice neighborhood.' "

The couple left in stunned silence. They never called again.

HOWARD AND I WERE PLEASED WITH RAY'S STORY. WE FIGURED Christopher had done the neighborhood a service. Anyone who didn't want to live next door to a pig was certainly not worthy of our town.

But meanwhile, the house seemed lonely for a family. Lilla and the girls would be a tough act to follow. There was not a day we didn't think of them. But they kept their promise and came to visit us every few months. One year, they surprised Howard on his birthday, and the next year surprised me on mine. They came up summers. And we visited them at the house they were renting in Connecticut—a huge '70s contemporary with cathedral ceilings and a deck and sliders.

Their new town was a different world, the girls told us. Practically no one had two parents; lots of kids were on Prozac; everyone was in therapy. Kate explained the social strata of the high school: there were the popular jocks and jockettes, the freaks, the poseurs (who pretended to be something they weren't), and the "froseurs" (fake poseurs, every week pretending to be a new different thing they weren't). The popular style was to dress up for school—no jeans and sweatshirts like in New Hampshire. One time when we stayed overnight, in the morning Kate emerged from her bedroom dressed for school in a miniskirt and fishnet stockings. Howard's bushy eyebrows shot up and nearly merged with his curly hair. Out of his mouth came words I had heard in my youth from my father, but which I'd never thought I'd hear from my own husband: "You are going to *school*," he asked, "dressed like *that*?"

Little girls no more, Kate and Jane were changing into beautiful young women. Yet they remained, in an important way, part of Hancock, part of our family, forever rooted to the joys of Pig Spa, of reading *Walker's Mammals* and dreaming of adventure with orcas and wolves and otters at our kitchen table. Jane was accepted at a private school that had its own zoo, where she particularly enjoyed caring for the captive emus. She excelled in art and biology. Kate, who had always struggled with dyslexia, now loved both reading and writing. Her reports on wildlife and essays about conservation and animal rights impressed her teachers. It was clear that both girls would grow up knowing how to find their bliss. They knew what bliss looked like: it looked like a black-and-white sleeping hog.

And to Chris they would always return. At first, because people's bodies, voices, and scents change so dramatically in adolescence, we wondered whether the pig would recognize his old friends when next he saw them. But even when many months went by between visits, Christopher always knew Kate and Jane. Each time they came, even before their hands touched him, Christopher issued the soft, blissful love grunts he always reserved just for them.

AT OUR HOUSE, WE FOUND THE REAL ESTATE MARKET RATHER *TOO* brisk. Since we'd bought the place, we'd enjoyed a parade of wonderful tenants—but they kept on leaving, and when they did it was always a crisis for us. We needed the rental income that tenants would bring, but since they actually lived *in* our house—which was also our workplace—anything but the perfect fit could be a disaster. The same year the Lillas left, we found ourselves in this uncomfortable position again.

Happily, Christopher Hogwood had always served as a litmus test for potential tenants. One trip to the barn made it clear that only pig lovers need apply. Mary Pat and John had considered Christopher a member of the family—despite the fact that the pig had nearly ruined her wedding dress. (She was carrying the dress, a Victorian drop-waisted confection made of handmade lace, home from the tailor's on a naked coat hanger, when Chris came rushing up to greet her with his muddy nose. She dashed with the dress to safety just in time.) After Mary Pat and John moved out, another couple had moved in. He was an artist, and she worked at the hospital in Keene, whose cafeteria issued regular if rather bland slops, which were ferried faithfully home. Then came a writer and jazz musician who worked at the Toadstool Bookshop in Peterborough. He turned part of the rental unit into a private-label beer-making enterprise, and gave the detritus of the process to a grateful Hogwood. Next, a fellow our age, with his white shepherd mix, moved in. They were refugees from a nasty divorce. One day he found that someone had left an unwelcome surprise on his doorstep—a plastic bag full of smelly garbage, with a tag that read FOR CHRIS. Our tenant's name happened to be Chris, too. He thought it was from his ex until we told him about the slops deliveries.

Now *this* tenant was leaving, and for the same reason everyone else had. We never raised the rent, and we assured all our tenants we would never kick them out. They all moved on because invariably, something wonderful happened to them. It was almost as if living in the house made wishes come true.

Mary Pat and John had moved to buy their own home in Peterborough and start a family, as did the couple who followed them. The beer-making bookseller left to live his dream as a poet, essayist, and musician, moving to New York City. And one day while our divorced tenant was driving to town, he met the love of his life when a slender, athletic woman and her horse crossed the street a mile and a quarter from our house. He left us to move in with her.

And this was just the sort of healing Selinda Chiquoine was seeking when she came to look at the apartment on the other side of our house on a gray day that next November.

Selinda and her husband, Ken, had what looked like an ideal life. They were just a year younger than us, with good jobs and wide interests and a beautiful new home surrounded with gardens in the woods in the next town over from us. Ken made great money as a computer scientist, and Selinda worked as a technical editor at a computer magazine.

Selinda had been trained as a geologist—she'd spent the summer before she graduated exploring a lead-zinc deposit in Alaska's Brooks Range, thirty miles north of the Arctic Circle. She'd lived with fifty-five others—only four of whom were women—in a tent with a plywood floor and a kerosene heater. Daily she helicoptered to work in the field, surveying the grid, sampling rocks, and measuring the angle of drill holes. When she married her college sweetheart, that put an end to her geology work. But Selinda, a petite, outgoing brunette with the brisk, cheery energy of a chipmunk, was quick to embrace a new outdoor passion—gardening. When the couple moved to Sharon, just a twenty-minute drive from our place in Hancock, Ken built her a ten- by thirty-foot greenhouse where she could grow flowers year-round.

But lately Selinda felt like she was foundering in a suburban housewife's life. She didn't really like her job at *Byte*. She wanted more time outdoors. She felt trapped. She and Ken weren't getting along. When they talked, they talked about computers. Then they argued, and the arguments solved nothing. She loved Ken but couldn't see a way to save the marriage. She felt the only thing to do was to move out.

Unfortunately, her options were limited. She didn't have a whole lot of money. Very few rental units would accept dogs—and she desperately wanted their two sixty-pound dogs, Reba and Louie, to live with her at least part of the time, as well as her cat, Tigger. Reba was a three-year-old black lab-setter mix, and Louie was a four-year-old white shepherd-lab mix. When she heard about our place, she was excited—and nervous. She didn't want to blow it.

Selinda was especially nervous about meeting Tess. She understood intuitively that it was important that Tess like her, and that Tess's opinion would inform our decision. Tess of course barked hysterically when Selinda came to the door, but after a toss of the Frisbee, she vacuumed Selinda with her nose. She approved.

Selinda didn't realize she was also going to be introduced to a pig whose opinion we considered equally astute. Next we went to the barn. Christopher grunted his approval.

Tess and Chris liked her. That was good enough for us.

So we showed Selinda the tenant's side of the house: the big living room and fireplace downstairs, the sunny kitchen/sitting room that used to be an enclosed porch, the old clawfoot bathtub the previous owners had painted pink, the slanted atticlike ceiling upstairs that made sleeping in the bedroom feel like a night in a tree house. Outside, I also pointed out a feature that perhaps other landlords might have skipped: Christopher and the chickens' manure pile. But I knew how to impress a gardener. Having a pig was like putting your compost on fast-forward.

Selinda was delighted. She loved our old white clapboard

farmhouse. She loved the porchlike feel of the south-facing apartment, and the way sunlight flooded in through the big windows. And she was *very* impressed with the manure pile.

I baked a carrot cake to welcome her when she moved in. It was a snowy day in January. But she was already thinking of the garden she would plant in the backyard come spring.

PEOPLE OFTEN ASKED US WHY WE'D NEVER HAD A GARDEN. For one, Howard was never interested. As for me, although I love all the plants on our property—the lilacs arching over the doorway, the great silver maple and its feathery neighbor, the tamarack tree, the perennial beds of phlox and hostas, the flowering quince and crab, the forsythia and the tall yellow Jerusalem artichokes by the barn—I've never tended a formal flower garden. I've never planted vegetables. Farmer Hogwood, however, unwittingly nurtured a squash and pumpkin crop: every year we noted a number of squash vines snaking out of the compost pile, recycling the bounty of the previous Halloween. Many of the species hybridized, and by first frost, we usually had enough weird vegetables for an attractive Halloween display by the front door—which we would then feed back to Chris again come winter. But even with New Hampshire's famously short growing season, I could never count on being here long enough to make the commitment to a real garden. And soon I would be journeying again.

While Selinda dreamed of gardens that winter, I dreamed of the jungle. For my next book, I was planning a series of expeditions to the Amazon. I had always wanted to visit this greatest of rain forests. My father had gone there several times, both while in the Army and then after he had retired from the shipping business and was working as a private consultant. In the '80s, he'd spent a week traveling the Peruvian Amazon on a boat, a pet capuchin monkey and a tame scarlet macaw on board. My mother had flown to meet him in Iquitos, and from there they traveled together to Brazil, to more civilized venues my mother would enjoy. But I know my father's favorite part. I have a wonderful picture from that South American trip in which he is holding a relaxed young three-toed sloth, its hairy arms and long claws reaching around his waist. My mother worried it would bite or scratch or pee on him. My father was beaming as if the sloth were the prize of the expedition, the most adorable and beautiful and unlikely creature on the planet.

For me, the Amazon was the ultimate Eden. The river embraces a jungle the size of the face of a full moon. With ten times more fish species than the Congo, electric eels that grow as long as limousines, and five thousand species of orchids, the Amazon's diversity dazzles; its vastness overwhelms. I always knew I would one day explore this richest of rain forests, but first, I would need an extraordinary guide to fathom it.

I had glimpsed that guide, oddly enough, in Sundarbans, on a day when the muddy waves opened and I saw into the future. There, in a tributary of the Ganges, I saw rising from the water the pinkish dorsal fins of three river dolphins. I saw them again and again on my travels there, brief glimpses only, but I never forgot them; sometimes they swam through my dreams. When I attended a marine mammals conference in Florida, I met a man who told me why.

He studied a different species of river dolphin, *Inia geoffrensis,* which lives in the Amazon. He told me the river people say these dolphins are shape-shifters. These dolphins can turn into people. They show up at dances (wearing hats to disguise the blowholes) and seduce men and women. And you must be careful, the river people told him, or the dolphins will take you away to the Encante, the enchanted city beneath the water—a place so beautiful, you will never want to leave.

I knew then what my next book would be: I would follow the pink dolphins of the Amazon. I wanted to follow them to Eden. I wanted to follow them to the Encante.

I wanted to follow them back, down, deep into the watery womb of the world, to the source of beauty and desire, to the beginning of all beginnings—and through their story, to show again the power of animals to transform us, to lead us home to Eden, and to remind us we can always start anew.

While Howard and I were eating dinner one night, Selinda knocked at the front door. Since she'd moved in, we visited often. We made cookies together, commuting with our baking sheets between ovens at opposite ends of the house. We canned jam, shared dinners, and sometimes went cross-country skiing with the three dogs on winter afternoons. The elegant Tess was disdainful and aloof among Selinda's rambunctious larger dogs. Howard nicknamed them Numskull (Reba) and Knucklehead (Louie) because they stole Tess's Frisbee, chased the wild turkeys that the neighbors fed with grain, and once ate an entire pan of fudge that a neighbor had set out to cool.

But this time Selinda had a request. "I was wondering," she asked, "if Howard would help me bring in a plant."

Selinda had transformed the rental unit into a cross between a greenhouse and a florist shop, with an excellent natural history library and some antique furniture from her grandmother's tossed in. I called her the Plant Goddess. She had well over a hundred leafy creatures crammed into the downstairs, drinking in the southern light: slipper orchids, purple shamrocks, bromeliads, jasmines, begonias, Amazon lilies, a tall jade plant, and at least thirty African violets. Potted plants hung from nails in the rafters, perched on plates by the windows, crowded the floor. Also, she usually had at least one vase of fresh flowers— Ken, from his lonely exile at their home, sent flowers every week. Selinda sometimes bought more at the local florist. She was always on the lookout for new plants, and seemed to be adding to her botanical collection every week.

"Oh—*I* can help you bring in a *plant*," I offered. How difficult could that be? But Selinda was adamant: "I think I really need *Howard*."

Howard was not delighted to have our dinner interrupted. But it was winter, and if the plant was not soon rescued from Selinda's car, it might freeze. He pulled on his parka and boots and trudged outside to see her latest prize. To his horror, he discovered a five-foot-tall tree lying on its side in her pickup. The sixteen-inch-diameter pot contained perhaps seventy pounds of soil. "If only we could harness Christopher to this job!" he said. But no; Chris would certainly have knocked the pot over, and then begun scattering the dirt with his nose. Besides, there was snow on the ground, and Chris did not like the feel of snow on his trotters for very long. Let outside, he'd run and push his snout through the snow, and then his feet would get all pink and cold and he'd rush back into his warm pen.

It was all Selinda and Howard could do to push the huge tree to the house through the snow in a wheelbarrow. Howard wrestled the thing to the front step, then onto the porch, then up another step through the door, fighting his way through the existing foliage in the hallway to install the new plant near an east-facing window in Selinda's kitchen.

This newest photosynthetic roommate was a tropical creature, a member of the same botanical family as the banana, Selinda explained. In fact, its leathery, blue-gray leaves were shaped like bananas. It had no flowers—yet. But it was the promise of these flowers that had made Selinda bring the huge, expensive plant home on a day when she had been feeling low. One day it would produce a riot of orange and yellow color, the spikes of its blooms splayed out like the crest of some imaginary tropical bird, opposite of which a bright blue tongue curved forth like a beak. The unborn but hoped-for flowers gave the plant its name: bird of paradise.

Paradise: the name evokes at once heaven and earth. It names a whispered longing; it tugs at our wishes and then spirits them away. Dictionary definitions imply that paradise is not of this life. Paradise is an afterlife, or a vanished Eden, or an idea that exists only in the minds of the holy men who wrote the texts of the great religions, an exhortation to a perfection we lost but still crave, or a promise of delight deferred. Paradise is what we want, and yet we are told that by definition we can't have it.

Ever since Sunday school, I'd been intrigued by the notion of Eden. It irritated my Methodist teachers that Eden appealed to me far more than heaven. Heaven you might get to after your death, if you were good—but there was no hope, I was told, of finding Eden. Heaven seemed boring, though. There is no mention of plants or animals there, whereas Eden was full of them. In Eden, the animals spoke (at least the snake did), and we understood what they said. In heaven you had to live in a building ("In my Father's house there are many mansions," Jesus said), and I wanted to live in a hollow tree. In Eden, there were not too many people (only two), whereas heaven sounded like it would be miserably crowded, considering everyone who thought they were going there. It would surely be even worse by the time I got there, if indeed I were headed that direction—of which my Sunday school teachers weren't so sure. To their dismay, I also stubbornly refused to blame the snake for all the trouble with Adam and Eve. I suspected God did, too. After all, He kicked the people out of Eden, but He let the snake stay.

Ever since we left that garden, we have been longing for Eden. It is a testament to human blindness that so few of us find it. "Heaven" wrote Thoreau, "is under our feet." Heaven, Eden, paradise, the Encante—call it what you will. It is as close as a backyard or a barnyard, and as extensive as the Amazon. Granted, in the Amazon, one might need a dolphin as a guide. But in Hancock, all you needed to point you to Eden was a good pig.

ONE DAY SHORTLY AFTER SHE ARRIVED, SELINDA BEGAN TO SUS-pect that the place she had chosen to live was very unusual indeed. She came home from work in Peterborough and noticed a pickup in the driveway. As she got out of her truck, she heard opera music coming from the direction of the barn—a wonderful tenor voice. She approached quietly. Harlow was singing the score from *The Gondaliers* to Christopher as he filled his dish with burned bagels, dill Havarti cheese, and cream of potato soup.

Several times each day, as she played in the yard with her dogs or collected firewood from the woodpile for the stove, Selinda's travels would bring her near the barn. Chris heard her footsteps and called to her: "Unh! Unhh! Nunhhh!" If she didn't come over, the calls reflected Christopher's growing irritation: "Unnnnhhhhh! Unnnnnhhhhhhhhhhh! Unhhhhh-hhhhhhhhhhhhhhhhhhhhh!"

Finally, if she still didn't come over, he would start banging the gate back and forth on its hinges with his nose, like a frustrated restaurant patron might bang a spoon trying to catch the ear of an inattentive waiter.

"OK! OK!" she'd call to him. "I'm coming!" Selinda was quickly trained not to leave the house without a carrot or an apple for Chris, or if there was none handy, to immediately swing by the grain bin and scoop up some pig and sow pellets to pour directly into his mouth. Except for orange peels and onions, she didn't save anything for the compost pile anymore. She fed it directly to Chris. And this, she realized, was in her own self-interest. As winter melted into mud season, as the March songs of returning phoebes and red-winged blackbirds gave way to the sleigh bell calls of the spring peepers in April and May, Selinda was counting the days till she could plant her garden.

THE GARDEN WAS EVERYTHING TO SELINDA. SHE IMAGINED IT IN her spare moments. She designed it in her head and on paper. From her second-story bedroom, she would look out at the area she would soon dig. Although she was still working at the computer magazine, in her mind, as she told me, "the garden was really what I was doing with my life at the time."

It was a garden with mostly annuals. She knew she wouldn't live at our house forever—though she was surely welcome to. It would be completely organic—no pesticides, no weed killers, no fertilizer other than Christopher's. The garden would supply much of the food we would eat that summer. But it was also a garden to feed the soul. "I want it to be a pretty garden to hang out in," she said. It would have not only vegetables, but also flowers and fragrant herbs: "I want it all!" she said. Even before she tilled its soil, the garden was "my world," as she put it, "my refuge."

The spot had been a garden once before. We remembered

our landlord's previous tenants had grown vegetables there. But after they left, it had reverted to grasses and goldenrods and ox eye daisies, indistinguishable from the rest of the un-mown field that stretched between the back lawn and the woods by Moose Brook.

When finally the threat of frost was past, Selinda began to till on June 1, as the wild strawberries began to bloom and the bobolinks first called. She pushed the heavy rototiller back and forth, back and forth, amid clouds of biting blackflies. It took Selinda three days to till the plot. The garden was enormous: twenty by fifty feet. We offered to help, but it was a one-person job. One person, that is, and one pig. From his tether, Christopher assumed the role of supervisor, following her work with great interest, ears forward, nostrils flared. The scents issuing from the freshly dug earth must have brought him a symphony of fragrance. Sometimes he called out to her to bring him something to eat. Often she couldn't hear him over the roar of the rototiller, but she knew he was there, and he was good, cheerful company. When she paused, she would bring him a handful of juicy weeds and pet his furry ears as he chewed.

And then it came time to plant. She had mapped out a circle of flowers in the middle: white narcissuses and low-growing twinkle phloxes, with daisylike calendulas and late-blooming dahlias toward the edge. A path ran around that circle, kept clear by cardboard under mulch to keep weeds out. Radiating from that circle were curved beds of lettuce. Irises would bloom in one corner and sunflowers rise from another. And there would be vegetables in abundance: arugula, chard, green peppers, Anaheim peppers, celery, spinach, green and wax beans, zucchini, carrots, cucumbers, and three kinds of tomatoes: Oregon Spring for sandwiches, plum tomatoes for canning, and cherry tomatoes for snacking. She planted herbs: scallions,

parsley, dill, and thirteen kinds of basil. And she grew pumpkins. They were just for Chris.

Over that summer, Selinda's garden gave us its all. Before
the Fourth of July, we were enjoying giant salads of peppery
arugula and buttery lettuce. By the end of the month, the dinners we ate under the silver maple often came directly out
of the soil: sauteed chard and red peppers, green and wax
beans with dill. By August we were wondering what to do
with all the zucchini—in a Methodist church cookbook, I even
found a recipe that used up two cups of the stuff in a chocolate
cake. (The cake was tasty but as heavy as lead.) As fall approached, Selinda made jar after jar of pesto to use up all the
basil. The fate of the pumpkins, however, was ensured from
the start.

What was perhaps most astonishing about Selinda's garden was that Christopher never invaded it. Our hens had no
qualms about hunting bugs there, which was actually a boon to
the plants and a strategy employed by many an organic gardener. Selinda's Reba and Louie would sometimes follow her
into the garden and step on her plants. Even Tess ran through
the garden once or twice, in pursuit of an errant Frisbee. Deer
occasionally visited to munch on the vegetables, as we could
see by their hoofprints in the soft soil. But why not our pig?

Because Selinda had maintained a border of tall grass
around her garden—a strategy that discourages certain bugs—
the garden could not be seen from a pig's eye view. But Christopher couldn't see the Amidon's lettuce garden down the road
either, and that never protected it from his incursions. Our pig
could certainly smell every ripening vegetable from throughout a huge range, one that might extend for miles. The olfac-
tory powers of animals are only now starting to be chronicled;
a wildlife biologist I know, Lynn Rogers, believes that bears,
for instance, may be able catch the scent of ripening hazelnuts

forty miles away. Pigs' sense of smell is legendary. They can even smell food underground, a talent people have exploited to locate prized truffles since Babylonian times. To this day, truffle pigs are still in service in the south of France, where they help to harvest the famous "black diamonds" of Périgord, which sell for up to $1,000 a pound. Sows are uniquely attracted to the scent of this truffle because it produces a steroid that is chemically identical to the testosterone present in the saliva of an amorous boar.

Christopher's path from the barn to the Pig Plateau took him within five yards of Selinda's garden. And while it's true that every morning when I let him out of the barn, and every evening when I'd put him back in, I ran ahead and lured him with fragrant, enticing slops, it remained a mystery why he never once visited the garden or violated its sanctity. He could have destroyed it in a quarter of an hour had he wished. But Selinda never worried about this. Christopher was her gardening buddy. There was no reason she could see that he should do anything but help her in her work.

By the end of the growing season, Christopher got his pumpkins, and Selinda had found her bliss. Through the long winter—through canning and Christmas cookies, through tedious hours at the computer magazine and snowy walks with the dogs—the seeds Selinda had planted that first spring in our backyard stayed alive. By the following spring, she knew what she would do: she would start her own landscaping company.

Other friends discouraged the new venture—starting a business is risky. But I'm not a risk-averse person; Howard and I encouraged her. Far too many of us cannot see the heaven under our feet, but Selinda had found hers. Go for it, we told her. She quit her job at the computer magazine and began gardening full time.

And as revelations often do, this one led to another. From

the moment she had moved in with us, Ken had unfailingly sent Selinda flowers every week. He was still courting his wife. Sometimes we saw him on the doorstep, a tall, slender blond with a handsome, eager face. In addition to the flowers, Ken took Selinda out to dinner each week. One day in late spring, she realized that her marriage was part of her bliss, too. After a year and a half living with us, she moved back in with her husband.

In our yard, Selinda's garden quickly grew over in wild-flowers and grasses, but every year the narcissus still blooms from its former center. And our friendship continues to flourish. Every summer we still put up blueberry jam together, and every winter we make Christmas cookies—only at Selinda and Ken's house, because the kitchen is much bigger over there. And several times a year, Selinda sends a special cutting to Howard: the spectacular, half-foot-long orange and blue blooms of her bird of paradise.

AFTER SELINDA LEFT, HALF OUR HOUSE WAS VACANT ONCE MORE. But at last, after standing empty for years, the Doll House again found a family.

When the real estate agent showed Bobbie Coffin the place, she laughed. Nobody knew where the septic system was—if one existed at all. Nobody was sure where the well was located. Much of the house was uninsulated. The kitchen needed to be redone. Bobbie and her husband, Jarvis, were already grandparents eight times over, and the thought of fixing up the old house at their age was just ridiculous. It was too much work.

They knew, because they'd done it before. They'd restored and repaired several old wooden houses in both Buffalo and Syracuse in upstate New York, where Jarvis brokered waste fibers to paper companies. They'd renovated the buildings, adopted dogs from the shelter, raised three boys, coaxed beautiful flowers and vegetable gardens from the clay soils—and raised chickens and pigs, too.

The pigs and chickens were Jarvis's idea, but Bobbie was a quick convert. When Jarvis brought home two not-yet-weaned pigs from an auction, Bobbie thought, "Oh my Lord! I've never had a pig before—how repulsive!" Within twenty-four hours she was bottle-feeding the pair, GubGub and Snooty. The next year, Jarvis went back to the auction and got three more piglets, to be co-owned by a syndicate of four of his friends. To Jarvis's dismay, once he got the pigs home, he discovered that one had a pronounced bulge under his tail. He consulted a vet and discovered he had bought what is known as a "busted pig." He was the victim of a sloppy castration: the pig had a hernia. The vet suggested they euthanize the animal.

But one member of the pig-owning syndicate happened to be the chief of pediatric surgery at Buffalo Hospital. "What are you talking about?" he said, when Jarvis related the vet's sobering news. "I fix those things every day!" The surgeon operated on the pig in a makeshift outdoor O.R. in Bobbie and Jarvis's backyard, using a plank and some sawhorses as an operating table. Jarvis (whose father was a doctor) acted as surgical assistant while the third member of the syndicate, the Episcopal bishop of western New York, looked on with interest. The pig, Benjamin, was fine in a week.

Those days were behind them now. They were looking for their retirement home. This would obviously not do at all. The old house would need careful restoration, as well as insulation. It was too small. They'd be uncomfortable. And then there was the question of the well and the septic system.

But then Bobbie stood in the street and looked at the sweet old house, with its white picket fence covered with antique roses. She imagined a vegetable garden in the backyard, an herb garden off the kitchen . . .

They bought the house. The only thing they would miss from their old life, they thought, would be raising the chickens and the pigs. They hated to be leaving that life behind.

But that was before they knew who was living in the barn next door.

CHAPTER 10

A HOG'S HOLIDAY

"HELLO, CHRISTOPHER! YOU'RE CERTAINLY LOOKING WELL today! Now, hold on—I *have* brought you something to eat, if you will just be *patient. . . .*"

Jarvis's cheerful, confident voice boomed into my office, answered by deep and appreciative grunting. Then came the crunching noise of the green apples that Jarvis had brought Christopher from the tree in the Coffins' front yard, fruit being ground into pulp. "Yes, ladies, I have something for you, too," Jarvis continued as the hens' interested queries swelled around him. Then came Jarvis's footsteps on gravel, the crunch of the metal scoop gathering cracked corn from the grain bin, and the happy clucks and mutterings of the chickens as they pecked at the feast our neighbor spread at their scaly feet.

I could hear the whole exchange on the baby monitor.

The baby monitor had been Bobbie's idea. Shortly after we had met, she and Jarvis had enthusiastically volunteered to look after Chris and the chickens whenever Howard and Tess and I went away, be it for an afternoon or a weekend. Having our hens visit their yard was one of Bobbie's deepest joys. She had adored her own little flock in upstate New York, the hens tended by a series of handsome and courageous roosters. Bobbie was thrilled to find friendly, clucking chickens back in her life again.

But, even though Bobbie had a far better view of our chickens from her house than we did from ours, she fretted about a fox attack. So she had set up the baby monitor she used when their youngest grandchildren visited, putting the transmitter by the Chicken Chalet and the receiver by her kitchen. Howard saw the wisdom of the device and bought one of our own. From that point on, with the receiver in my office, I wrote my books and articles to an edifying fugue of clucks, cackles, and grunts.

"What do you suppose they are saying?" I would ask Howard at lunch. "Maybe they are saying something really brilliant and I'm just missing it." One day I thought I could almost make it out:

"Eeee! Eeee! Eeeee! Eeequals! M C squared!"

It was Howard down by the transmitter.

There were times I had to turn the thing off. Sometimes, when a chicken cackled with particular enthusiasm, Tess would break out barking in alarm. But even with the monitor silent, I didn't much worry about the hens. Bobbie and Jarvis would watch out for them.

They took our animals' safety and comfort seriously. One

time we returned from a three-day trip to find that Jarvis had built the Ladies all new, super-snug nest boxes. Another time, he rebuilt their perches, offering different shapes and thickness so each hen could choose the perch best suited to her individual comfort.

Bobbie and Jarvis were the perfect grandparents—to their children's children, and to our animals. Slender, beautiful Bobbie was always giving the hens little treats. When Bobbie and Jarvis would visit the barn, Chris would greet them as soon as he heard their distinctive footsteps striding over the stone wall. Jarvis and Bobbie visited Chris and the hens so often that Jarvis built a wooden walkway over the boggy area (which proved to be the location of the mysterious septic system) between their yard and ours. The barn became a destination for their grandchildren to visit, and feeding their table scraps to Chris and the chickens became a family tradition, just as it had been with the Lillas.

One summer day the Coffins brought Christopher a bonanza. The couple had returned from the annual Republican party picnic (a pig roast, I learned to my dismay), where bushels of roasted corn and baked potatoes had gone uneaten. Jarvis and Bobbie had packed up all the leftovers in huge food coolers, loaded the bounty into their car, and then—in a feat that amazed me, even though I knew our stocky, barrel-chested neighbor was immensely strong—Jarvis had somehow carried them about three hundred yards from their car to the woodpile by Christopher's pen. Even though Howard and I were Democrats, we couldn't say the Republicans never did anything for us. This was true pork-barrel politics.

Bobbie and Jarvis's motives, though, couldn't have been purer. One day Jarvis made a laminated sign and put it up on our barn. It was a quote from St. Francis of Assisi, patron saint of animals: "Not to hurt our humble brethren is our first duty to them, but to stop there is not enough. We have a higher mission: to be of service to them whenever they require it."

I loved the quote, and loved that Jarvis had put it there. For me, the saint's words rang true far beyond our barnyard: they named the reason for the work that carried me around the world, and the force that drew me back home again.

I didn't realize then that Jarvis did not put up the sign for my benefit alone. It was for him and Bobbie, too. Not until years later would I fully understand why tending to Christopher gave our neighbors such special satisfaction.

But perhaps I should have guessed: satisfaction was our pig's specialty. The word owes its roots to the Old French for "to make full." That certainly described the goal of Christopher's eating career, but more than that, it described his effect on the hearts and lives of his closest companions.

OUR PIG-O-METRIC MEASUREMENTS REVEALED THAT BY THE END of the first year that Jarvis and Bobbie were in residence, Christopher had topped seven hundred pounds.

"Will he ever stop growing?" people asked us. We thought so—eventually. But we weren't sure. A few animals, including sharks, spiders, and lobsters, grow throughout their lives. Sharks can grow endlessly because their skeletons are made of cartilage, not bone, and they live in the weightless environment of the oceans. Spiders and lobsters, as well as many other invertebrates, can keep growing because they wear their skeletons on the outside; they can simply shed them when they get bigger. But most of us with internal skeletons, like people and pigs, must stop growing at some point. With Chris, we didn't know when that point would come. We didn't know when he had passed the porcine equivalent of adolescence. We didn't know when he might enter middle age—possibly he was there now. But if you can't guess the end, how do you find the middle? We still had no idea how long a pig might live. *Walker's Mammals* said that the average longevity for wild pigs was about ten years. But I knew of one sow at a children's petting zoo who was said to be nearly twenty. Whenever I met veterinarians, I asked them what they knew of this. Most felt a pig ought to live as long as a dog. But a few wondered if one might live as long as do some of their fellow ungulates—a cow can live to be twenty, and a horse, with luck, can make it past thirty.

So few people have allowed pigs to live long enough to answer these questions. We were on the cutting edge of knowledge in this department.

We knew for certain, though, that Christopher Hogwood was not the biggest pig who had ever lived—not by a long shot. The heaviest pig on record was named Big Bill, a Poland China hog owned by Burford Butler of Jackson, Tennessee. The Poland China breed, with its droopy ears, black body, and white snout, tail, and socks, was originally developed for its ability to produce lard. When Big Bill was measured in 1933, he stood five feet tall at the withers, measured nine feet long, and weighed 2,552 pounds. His belly dragged on the ground.

We didn't particularly want our pig to weigh more than our car. Seven hundred pounds seemed a nice, round number, and Christopher, at age seven, seemed a nice, round pig. He was about five and a half feet long, and when he was standing on all fours, the top of his head reached about three feet high. We thought that was about perfect. We thought Christopher's weight had finally reached its zenith.

But that was before the ice storm of '98.

I WAS IN WASHINGTON, D.C., WHEN IT HIT, WORKING ON A FILM for National Geographic. Two years earlier, a film crew from its *Explorer* TV program had come with me to Sundarbans to make a documentary on the tigers and the villagers' wisdom, and they had asked me to write the script. Now I had another idea. A wildlife rehabilitator friend of mine, Ben Kilham, was raising three orphaned black bear cubs near his home in central New Hampshire in an unusual and important new way. He was not raising them like a person typically raises baby animals, but like a mother bear raises her cubs—by spending ten hours a day in the woods with them. In the process, he was getting an extraordinarily intimate insider's view of what life is like for American black bears. I proposed the idea over the phone, and as usual, our cockatiel was sitting on my head. I had taught her to whistle the National Geographic theme song, and the idea occurred to me that the folks at the organization's top echelon might like to hear this. She whistled it on request—and, charmed, the executives quickly agreed to back the bear project.

We'd filmed Ben and the cubs off and on for nearly two years as the babies grew to maturity. Now I was writing the script as the producer and the editor crafted the final sequences. One night—January 8—we flicked on the TV at the producer's Georgetown house, where I was staying, and to our surprise found New Hampshire on the news.

The television showed a glazed landscape, naked branches of the trees like glass figurines, pines slumped under the weight of the ice, beech limbs shorn in half. Everywhere were fresh, bright wounds of broken wood, and trees piled on top of trees and telephone poles and power lines.

The state was in the grip of a crippling storm. About half of New Hampshire lost power, and it was predicted that in some areas it would not be restored for weeks.

I phoned Howard, hoping he'd be able to pick up the phone.

At our house, he told me, we'd lost power for only a few

hours. Bobbie and Jarvis had power, too. But on the other side of town, the damage was far worse. You could smell pine pitch everywhere. People heard trees falling, like explosions, every thirty seconds all night long. Walking in the woods was like walking through six inches of ice cubes. Howard called it the "have and have-not" storm. On the other side of town, folks had to move in with friends or relatives or were living by candlelight with heat from the woodstove. For days after the storm, that side of town had no electricity.

It did not take us long to realize the consequences. Far from a natural disaster, the ice storm was a hog's holiday: soon the melting contents of Hancock's best-stocked refrigerators and freezers began to make their way toward Christopher's sty.

Over the next week, food came by the bucket. Food came by the bag. Mary Garland brought a huge plastic garbage can full, which Howard somehow helped her wrestle out of her car trunk and onto the lawn. It was an astounding boon. Mary is a retired interior designer with impeccable taste, known to throw lavish parties at the last minute (and make them look effortless) and always ready to welcome her many children and grandchildren for impromptu visits. Once I opened her cupboard looking for a glass and found no fewer than four huge bottles of premium balsamic vinegar sitting there, back when no one even knew what balsamic vinegar was. You can imagine the contents of her fridge and freezer.

Now they belonged to Chris.

After the ice storm, our pig got his usual quota of banana peels and celery stalks. But now there were melting quarts of Ben and Jerry's ice cream. Frozen blueberries hand-picked the previous summer. Brie and Camembert wrapped in puff pastry. Entire frozen lasagnas, Sarah Lee chocolate cakes, frozen eclairs, huge slabs of smoked fish, tubs of crème fraîche ...

At last Chris had achieved pig paradise: his bowl overflowed. For most of his life, we had pretty much given him whatever slops we could get. We seldom got a whole bucket of slops for every day of the week, and we usually supplemented this with grain. But now, he actually had more than he could possibly eat. And he knew it.

For us, however, Christopher's astonishing fortune created an almost oxymoronic problem. When I came home from my stint in Washington, I found Howard and I were now the guardians of a picky pig.

Food items once relished were now disdained. He pushed a cabbage away with his snout like a toy ball. He ignored mushroom stems, celery stalks, and broccoli stems. This went on for months. Come summer, he wouldn't bother with corn husks. He preferred his corn fresh, on the cob, and buttered.

Thank goodness we had Fiddleheads Café. Just a year after Harlow sold his cheese shop and retired, a young local couple opened a gourmet eatery and catering business even closer to us, on Hancock's Main Street. They generously in-structed their staff to sort their kitchen garbage in accordance with Christopher's all-vegetarian, no-citrus, no-onion prefer-ences. Daily we'd pick up the slops buckets from the kitchen. Lifting the lid, out wafted the scent of vinaigrette, homemade pasta or rice salad, imported olives, and smoked Gouda. On Mondays, Fiddleheads was closed, so on Sundays we would get all the leftover pastries: blueberry and poppyseed and ba-nana muffins, cinnamon rolls, cherry, lemon, and cheese Dan-ish. Quite frequently, we would go to weddings and receptions in town that the café catered to find that at these elegant events we were eating the same thing as our pig. The presentation was different: for us, the spanakopita triangles would be on a pretty tray, while in Chris's slops bucket they might be floating in pancake batter, with strawberry caps piled on top, perhaps topped with a dollop of leftover artichoke dip.

Still, we would sometimes end up with something in the bucket he wouldn't eat. Occasionally some well-meaning soul would bring us a bucket of green leek tops or a couple of aging cabbages. We'd thank them and then dump it in the compost pile. There, sooner or later, the chickens would eventually find and discuss it, and I could hear the whole exchange on the baby monitor.

But Christopher had made his desires known. We simply obeyed, as was our mission and our privilege. And for this, he rewarded us with a rare, uplifting spectacle. Howard and I were happy—but always longed for a wider readership, for our words to change the world. Tess was happy—but always wished we could spend most of the day playing with the Frisbee. But Christopher was another story. Here was a soul whose every wish, beyond his wildest dreams, had been utterly and completely satisfied.

"Now THERE IS NO POINT OF VIEW FROM WHICH A REALLY CORPU-lent pig is not full of sumptuous and satisfying curves," the British novelist and essayist G. K. Chesterton wrote in *The Uses of Diversity* in 1920. It was Chesterton's boyhood dream to own a pet pig, he confessed in this book. "I could never imagine why pigs should not be kept as pets," he wrote. "To begin with, pigs are very beautiful animals. Those who do not think so do not look at anything with their own eyes but through other people's eyeglasses."

What other creature could so satisfy the eye? "You can look down on a pig from the top of the most unnaturally lofty dogcart," Chesteron exalted. "You can examine the pig from the top of an omnibus, from the top of the Monument, from a balloon, or an airship, and as long as he is visible, he will be beautiful. . . . In short, he has that fuller, subtler and more universal kind of shapeliness which the unthinking . . . mistake for a mere absence of shape. For fatness itself is a valuable quality."

Fatness, Chesterton suggested, bestows satisfaction on the onlooker by proxy: fatness is evidence of satisfaction itself—satisfaction, if you will, made flesh.

Here in the United States, we worship the svelte and the fit. Fat is decried as evidence of sloth and greed. But other cultures see things differently.

Unlike Chesterton, I had never truly appreciated the beauty of fat until my first journey to the pink dolphins in Brazil. In Manaus—a city a thousand miles inland, where the two major tributaries, the tannin-stained Rio Negro and the milky Rio Solimoes meet to form the Amazon—fat is celebrated. Manaus revels in the ripeness of flesh and fat. It's not that its inhabitants are fatter than North Americans—they're definitely not. The difference is that they like to show it off. The women—even pregnant, even old, even grossly obese—all seem to wear tight stretch pants and clingy halter tops and short, tight dresses, or jeans popping at the seams, often with the top button undone to accommodate the overflow. In the fish market, the big bellies of bare-chested old men spill over the waistbands of their pants like the foaming head on a beer. The people there appreciate strength and fitness, I thought, but they remember, too, that many people in their country are still hungry. Fat is abundance. Fat is fecundity. Fat is the fullness of life.

Christopher, I thought, would have loved the Amazon. I often saw pigs there, sometimes riding calmly with their people in canoes. Brazil had lots of food. Even the trees that lined the city streets spilled their fruits with lush abandon onto the sidewalks: mango, guava, papaya. The same was true of music: samba, rock, and boi gushed lavishly into the street from stores, buses, and restaurants, spraying notes like the waters of a public fountain. In the rainy season, when my photographer and I arrived on our first expedition, every living creature seemed caught up in the sensuous savor of life. In India, they call this *rasa:* the sweet sap, the juicy life essence, the core satisfaction in the enjoyment of life, be it food or art or sex.

Never before had I fallen so instantly under the spell of a place. To me, even the sound of human voices was alluring: Brazilian Portuguese seemed spoken through lips numbed from kissing. No wonder they believed that the shape-shifting pink dolphins could seduce you. The Amazon certainly seduced me.

In fact, each of my four expeditions there was uniquely enchanted. The first day out on the water ended in a storm of pink lightning—like some message, some promise, from the pink dolphins themselves. On my second trip, this time to Peru, I met Gary Galbreath, an evolutionary biologist to whose vast knowledge and kind soul I was drawn like a starving person to a gigantic fruiting tree. He showed me how to time-travel, journeying to the prehistoric past, when the hairy, lumbering ancestors of dolphins walked on land and then transformed themselves into creatures so perfectly suited to water. And more gifts from him were in store: although I didn't know it at the time, my next big book, as well as two others I wrote for children, was born from our meeting in the Amazon.

As if casting a spell, the strange, primitive, bulbous-headed pink dolphins completely captured my heart. I followed them every way I could: I followed them back in time. I tried to follow them with radio telemetry. I followed them into the spirit realm, drinking ayahuasca, a hallucinogenic brew, under the guidance of a shaman to commune with the powers of the waters. I followed them through the people's stories, the myths about the shape-shifting dolphins who transform into humans and seduce people at dances, luring them into the enchanted underwater world, the Encante.

And on my last trip to the Amazon, I joined the dolphins there. Along the blue-water Rio Tapajós, in the Brazilian state of Pará, along a deserted white-sand beach I would swim each day a quarter mile out into the river. There I would hang in the water, nearly crazy with anticipation—and seven wild pink dolphins would appear as if by magic and swim around me. I could feel the currents their bodies made as they slipped through the water. Sometimes a dolphin would pull its bulging head from the water, and its gray eyes would focus on mine. Inside those clear blue waters, surrounded by pink dolphins, I felt engulfed in ecstasy.

Again and again, when local people learned I was swimming with dolphins, they cautioned with the same phrase: *"Cuidado com o boto"*—be careful of those dolphins, for everyone knows they can sweep you away, seduce you to the Encante. And yes, I knew well the pull of that desire. Again and again in my work I would follow some new animal, pour out my soul, and fill myself utterly with the graces and sorrows, the mysteries and truths, of some new place.

"How can you go to all these difficult, dangerous jungles?" people often asked me. To me, the travel was a joy. It didn't matter that there were piranhas in the water, or that my skin burned so badly it blistered, or that ants crawled into my bed at night to drink the fluid from the blisters and feast on my dead skin. To be with the dolphins filled my heart; there was no room for discomfort or fear.

But to merely travel is not enough. Few people understand that the heroism is in the writing. To bring the stories of these places back, to share the truths amassed by those who live close to the Earth, to help us remember how to keep the earth whole—that is the difficult part. The real work, the real transformation, takes place at my desk in New Hampshire, surrounded by the familiar animals I love. To make sense of the Encante, to make use of its magic, I needed the anchoring fulfillment of home.

BACK IN HANCOCK, THOUGH, TROUBLE WAS BREWING IN PIG Paradise.

Some six months after the ice storm, Christopher had trouble rising to his feet. He would rock and rock but couldn't seem to get his legs under him. Alarmed, I phoned Chris's vet, Tom, whom we hadn't seen since the tuskectomy—and discovered he had quit the large-animal portion of his practice. I called Tess's vet, Chuck DeVinne, for a reference. Instead, he came to see Christopher himself.

Unbeknownst to me, Chuck had a fair amount of experience with pigs: attending Bethany College in West Virginia, he had befriended a five-hundred-pound pig, a professor's pet who wandered freely around campus. Between college and vet school he'd even worked as a herdsman on a farm with dairy cattle and fifty Yorkshire hogs. He met an even bigger pig there—a boar who was perhaps seven years old. One of Chuck's first management decisions on the farm was to give that fellow to someone else as a pet—he weighed too much to safely breed the younger sows without crushing them.

Chuck had met many pigs since then. But Christopher, now nine, was the oldest pig he had ever seen, and certainly one of the biggest. With one glance, Chuck made his diagnosis: at more than seven hundred pounds, Christopher Hogwood was overweight.

How could Chuck tell?

"The body shape," Chuck said. "The profile. You should

be able to look at them and see the definition of the spine, the flank." But Christopher was, as he delicately put it, "somewhat . . . amorphous." The extra weight was just too much on his aging joints.

Just how fat was Chris? He was not actually *obese*, I was relieved to hear. Our pig was better off than nearly half of American adult humans, who are 30 percent overweight or more, and thus at increased risk for heart trouble, diabetes, and stroke. Chris was, proportionally, about half that fat— about 15 percent overweight. He was more like the average, middle-aged guy who could stand to lose twenty pounds or so.

Except in Christopher's case, he had to lose about a hundred.

THE HORROR, THE HORROR! OUR PIG ON A DIET! WHAT COULD BE more unfair? At first I was overwhelmed by the prospect of separating Chris from his food—his muse, his bliss, his Higher Power. But Chuck helped me to see that I really had no choice: if Christopher was too fat, he could not stand up to enjoy his meals in the first place. It was a circular argument, as rotund as Christopher himself, and one I could not refute.

Howard and I conferred. Would Chris have to go on special low-cal pig chow? (No such thing exists.) Should we model his diet on something like Weight Watchers? (Would it work without a support group?) Many of my human friends were familiar with the diet dilemma and offered their advice. Gretchen swore by Atkins, but we agreed that it wouldn't work well for a vegetarian pig. Besides, carbs were his favorites. Liz had gotten svelte on a diet that featured prepackaged shakes, meals she referred to as "swill." Well, swill would be fine with Chris. The question was, how much?

Whatever diet we decided upon, if it was successful, my

women friends agreed that I would need to share it with the world: the "My Pig Lost One Hundred Pounds on This Diet" diet. The slogan: "If a pig can lose, you can too." Liz joked that finally I would have a best-seller. American women would flock to it.

Except this book would have only one sentence. What finally worked for Chris was simple: one bucket of slops a day.

He still got at least two *meals* a day—they were just smaller. He still enjoyed his favorite, luscious treats. He still enjoyed a varied, gourmet menu. He simply got less of it. I slowed the flow of slops from everyone but Fiddleheads. To try to make up for the smaller portions, I fed Chris more slowly: anything that wasn't too sticky, I fed him by hand, announcing each morsel as I fished it out of the bucket.

"What do we have here?" I would ask, plucking a crumbling yellow square out of a gooey mix of mushroom soup and pancake batter.

"Unnnhh?" he would query, the lilt of his grunt rising like lifted eyebrows.

"A *delicious* piece of cornbread!" I'd announce.

"Unhhhhhhhh!" he'd answer—and I would place the item in his opened mouth. As he chewed, I would toss the Frisbee for Tess, and then fish for the next treat. "And how about a piece of . . . what? Moussaka? Vegetable lasagna? You tell me."

"Unh. Unh. Unh."

And so it went. Pick, toss, feed. Talk, grunt, chew. The clucks of the hens, the jangle of Tess's tags as she brought back the Frisbee, the narration of the menu and its reception—I didn't realize it, but Howard liked to listen in on the baby monitor.

The feedings were long. They were messy. And they were deeply satisfying for us both. Though I gave Chris less food, he showed me how to appreciate each mouthful's sensuous savor.

And as Hogwood's weight slowly dropped, his joints improved. The next time Chuck came by, he said he thought Chris was mighty spry for his age.

I feel sure that Chris would have preferred more food rather than less. This was one of the few times when I had the upper hand. In most other disagreements we had, the pig prevailed. And that was a good thing—because most of the time, he was right.

It was the last day of August—an achingly beautiful, golden day when the air throbbed with cricket song and buzzed with dragonfly wings and smelled like ripening apples.

This was the sort of day you ought to be outside. Howard and I were admittedly driven—but at least we recognized such times. To me, days like this one were holidays—the word owes its origin to "holy days," and I felt it a sacred duty to honor them. Even if it meant having to work till nine every night all the rest of the week, and both days of the weekend, on these brilliant, extraordinary days, we'd try to take an afternoon hike with Tess, or steal a few hours watching the loons at our favorite pond. Our friend David Carroll, a turtle expert, artist, and author who lived an hour's drive away, called this practice "keeping an appointment with the season." When the salamanders woke for their mass matings on the first warm rainy night in April, when the spotted turtles emerged from hibernation in March, on the moonlit nights when the wood turtles nest in June—well, David just had to be there, no matter what. I sometimes joined him. One appointment for which I was willing to drop everything was the ripening of the blueberry crop in August. Selinda and I would spend hours picking gallons of them, enough for blueberry pie and blueberry muffins and blueberry pancakes and blueberries on breakfast cereal, and we'd freeze the rest to make blueberry jam later, which we'd give as Christmas gifts. Howard branded ours "Hogwood's Choice: The Jam Hogs Would Choose if Hogs Had a Choice," and I made labels for the jars with a big rubber stamp.

But lately, too many gorgeous days had slipped by. Our schedules had been crazy for years now. Howard was still promoting his last book, getting ready for publication of another, and circulating a proposal for a new one, which he was researching that very day at the library in Keene. I was at the point when I didn't have time to cut my toenails, much less scrub the toilet, and dog hair rolled like tumbleweed through the house. I was now writing for film and for radio, for adults and for children. I'd researched my first children's book—written for fourth through eighth graders, the age Kate and Jane were when I met them—in a pit full of eighteen thousand red-sided garter snakes in Manitoba. (And what were they doing in there? Copulating in huge mating balls of up to two hundred individuals—a scene I was confident would delight children as much as it appalled adults.) That same year I'd made my four expeditions to the Amazon and filmed *Mother Bear Man*. Now I was developing proposals for more kids' books as well as a new project that would take me with Gary Galbreath on a quest to find a mysterious golden bear in Southeast Asia.

So on this heartbreakingly beautiful day, I was stuck in my little downstairs office. None of the work I was doing was creative. It was all detail work, phone calls and e-mails and editing. I felt chained to the computer. At least Christopher could enjoy the sun. So I went to let him out to bask in the sun at the Pig Plateau.

But Christopher had other plans.

When I swung open the gate, Christopher stepped out eagerly. But he showed no interest in the can of grain I shook. He started off in the wrong direction—*away* from the Pig Plateau and toward the house. Quickly I ran to grab a slops bucket, featuring marinated wild rice and cubes of Gouda cheese, stale bagels and noodles in Thai peanut sauce. But he wasn't interested in this either. Unbeknownst to me, one of Jarvis and Bobbie's grandchildren had just fed him a bucket of apples. Christopher wasn't the least bit hungry.

He wasn't in a hurry, either. He did not seem compelled by any particular errand. Christopher Hogwood was out for a stroll—a situation akin to a bulldozer running rampant through the neighborhood. He tore up a portion of lawn the size of a throw rug.

"No, no, no, Chris! Don't do that!" I cried. "Stop, stop!" Chris could not possibly fathom what about his activity displeased me, possibly because the entire idea of the lawn is patently absurd. People see a lawn as something you water and mow, and in too many cases fertilize and poison. Christopher's view was far saner. Grass was for eating, smelling, and rooting.

After excavating a roughly pig-sized hole, Christopher, seeming to heed my vehement protest, continued on his jaunt. He walked up toward the house, and touched it with his nose, causing a clapboard to spring from the wall.

"No, no! This is dreadful! You dreadful beast, leave the wall alone!"

Christopher looked up at me as if I were insane, and said, "Unh." His grunt spoke volumes: "All right. Be that way. I'll find something else to do." He took a few more steps—and then effortlessly bit off a wooden plank from the back porch.

"No, no, Pig Man! Come on, let's go to the Plateau!"

I didn't have time for this. I was thinking of the list of office chores on my desk. Phone calls. E-mails. Correcting some galleys. I was behind on my *Globe* column. I owed National Public Radio a commentary.

But Christopher obeyed a higher calling: the intoxicating call of green grass and sunshine, the sweet scent of the earth on one of the last days of summer.

He wandered across the backyard, pausing to push his nose disk into the lawn here and there and creating foot-deep divots. He headed slowly toward the fenced field, which at the moment was bereft of visiting horses. With the tip of his nose, effortlessly he swung open the gate, which I can't even lift, and entered the pasture.

Lazily, Christopher began to stroll across the four-acre field. At the other end was Route 137. I had to stop him. Grain wouldn't work; slops wouldn't work. There was only one thing left to do.

As I walked beside him, I began to rub his belly and grunt our favorite mantra: "Good, good pig. Big, good pig. Fine, fine swine. Good . . . good . . . good." He crumpled to the ground and rolled over in porcine bliss. And then I lay down beside him beneath an apple tree. As long as I lay there and stroked him, he wouldn't get up and leave. And that was how I spent that afternoon: lying beside someone I loved, watching the clouds and the dragonflies and the sun streaming through the leaves of the apple tree.

It was a little unplanned holiday in the middle of the work week. Some say happiness lands lightly on you, like a butterfly. Sometimes this is so. But sometimes happiness comes lumbering toward you, like a fat, satisfied pig—and then thuds, grunting, by your side.

"THERE'S A BIG BLACK-AND-WHITE SPOTTED PIG ON OUR LAWN." The Sunday morning phone call was resoundingly familiar. "Is it yours?"

Minutes before the phone rang, I had returned from feeding Christopher his breakfast in his pen. He didn't break out much anymore. Howard said Chris reminded him of a major league baseball manager: "You know, those men who gravity is pulling toward a pear shape, but who still must dress in a young man's uniform. When they head out of the dugout to talk to their pitcher, they come trotting out, maybe trying to match pace with a younger pitching coach—but once they hit the foul line, they break into a walk."

Our pig was like that now. No longer did he shoot out of

his pen like a snorting cannonball. He trotted out sometimes. More often he stepped out. And sometimes he had to be coaxed. Once out, he might wander, but seldom far. That he would be visiting *these* callers was extremely unlikely: Bud and Sarah Wilder lived over a mile away, over by the apple orchard, up a long, steep hill.

For once, I could pretty confidently reply that no, it must be some other pig.

In fact, it was. Howard and I rushed over to offer a pig assist and found on the Wilders' lawn a beautiful, young Gloucestershire Old Spot, a rare but venerable western English breed with distinctive heavy, drooped ears. Her name was Annabelle, and she belonged to the Primianos, who lived just down the road from the Wilders. Annabelle ate grass happily, as if she was just passing time as she waited for the Primianos to come pick her up in their trailer.

Although I still considered Christopher the epitome of porcine beauty (and I even preferred his tall, furry ears to Annabelle's pretty floppy ones), I envied Annabelle her youth. Christopher was now an elder statesman. At age ten, he had passed what *Walker's Mammals* had said was the average length of a pig's life. We had never learned for sure how long a pig could live, but Chris had certainly outlived all his littermates by nine and a half years.

With the graces of porcine seniority also came some of the ailments of old age. Though his diet had lessened the stress on his joints, now he had real arthritis. Chuck had us treating it with a pelleted, molasses-flavored horse version of the dietary supplement for joint health, glucosamine, and with the equine painkiller phenylbutazone, which we gave him with his meals twice a day. Because the bute could upset his stomach, we also gave him antacids—in huge quantities. On his rare expeditions to the discount chain store in Keene, Howard would pick up twenty packages of the stuff. ("You'd think the clerk at the cash register would ask, 'Hey, are you OK?'" he once reflected. But no; this was a chain store and Keene was the big city.) Each morning and evening, I would stuff all Christopher's medications into a pastry from Fiddleheads—and if we were out of pastries, I would make peanut butter and drug sandwiches.

Christopher had also developed what we called porcine pattern baldness. It wasn't on his head, but the bald spot occupied an increasing amount of real estate between his neck and his shoulders. Chuck took skin scrapings to see if it was some sort of mite or disease, but it was not. It was the same sort of skin problem that older people tend to get.

In fact, pigs are so like us that we are prey to many of the same ailments. When Chris was twelve, he suffered what is known in people as a transient ischemic attack, or mini-stroke. I was able to recognize it immediately, because only weeks before, the same thing had happened to Tess.

One June morning, as we were just waking up, she'd fallen over. At first I thought it was *her* arthritis. By then Tess was fourteen, and between her age and the damage from her youthful collision with the snowplow, some mornings she was stiff and would sometimes limp or trip. But then I saw her eyes—she was dazed, as if drunk. I phoned Chuck at home, where we were always welcome to call. He said to immediately give her three baby aspirins. Later she came in for blood work to make sure that no organs had been damaged; they were not. When we came home, we were so terrified and exhausted by the ordeal that we slept through the rest of the day. But the next morning, ever cheerful, she was playing with her ball.

The same thing happened to Christopher that same summer—except on a larger scale. One Sunday morning, he didn't want to get up. When I finally urged him to his feet, his huge head was cocked eerily to the side. One pupil was large, the other small, and he swayed on his trotters so badly I feared he would fall. When I couldn't reach Chuck, Liz came rushing over. We calculated the proper dose of aspirin for a seven-hundred-pound pig from what Chuck had prescribed for a thirty-pound dog and hid the pile of aspirin in chocolate chip cookies. Chris had dramatically improved by the next morning, just like Tess.

We knew how lucky we were. Our animals were now roughly the same biological age as our parents. Howard's mom and dad had both been through cancer scares but were now fine. My mother had high blood pressure and other circulatory problems, but she was still active, enjoying church, the sewing circle, and ladies' functions, living on her own, presiding over the five-bedroom house in Alexandria. We were acutely aware that age has its hazards—but that old age can also be rich, vibrant, and long. We had Liz's mother, Lorna, as our example.

At age ninety-seven, she had finally moved in with Liz and Steve. She could still drive, and unlike many of the elderly residents of our town, she never hit anything; but her joints hurt sometimes, and walking the flight of stairs to her bedroom at the big old Cambridge house was getting to be a chore. Lorna published her last book at age one hundred; Liz and Steve rented a tent and held a huge publication party in the backyard, and borrowed a lion cub and an adolescent tiger from a private zoo to mix with the guests, who had come from as far away as Australia to attend the celebration. Lorna entertained a fairly constant stream of visitors and admirers thereafter—until the night a few years later when she spoke her last, loving words. "Bless you," she said to Liz. And then she closed her eyes and died peacefully at home, surrounded by those she loved, just a few weeks short of her 104th birthday.

Although they were aging, our animals were in relatively

fine fettle. Tess still charmed visitors with her athleticism and wit. She still had more energy than anyone we knew. She still leaped to catch the Frisbee. She still anticipated our every move. No matter what time of day, and absent any visual clues that we could discern, Tess knew when we were going to the top part of the barn for a rake or shovel, and got there ahead of us. She knew, long before we made the turn toward the bottom floor of the barn, when we were going to see Chris and the chickens instead. She still did everything a person could ask of her, usually before we even uttered our wishes aloud.

But then, one day, distracted by an interesting smell, Tess dropped her Frisbee in the tall grass. Usually when this happened, all Howard had to do was remind her, in a normal conversational voice and without pointing, where her toy was, and she would go pick it up. This time she stared at him blankly. Then we realized that Tess was deaf—and probably had been for months.

Christopher continued to amass appreciative acolytes for Pig Spa. He had acquired new devotees when the Miller-Rodat family moved from Los Angeles and bought a house in town. Mutual friends introduced us to Mollie and Bob because Bob Rodat had written the script to one of my favorite films, *Fly Away Home,* about orphaned geese whose adoptive parent, a pilot, flies along with them on their first migration; later Bob wrote *The Patriot, Saving Private Ryan,* and many others. Howard's and my claim to fame? We had a giant pig. We quickly made a date for Chris to meet Mollie and Bob's sons. Jack was seven and Ned four.

Chris made a huge impression. Jack wowed his first-grade class with the August 25 entry from his "Summer Fun Journal": "Today," he wrote, "we went to feed our friend Christopher Hogwood. The same day Christopher escaped. He ran around the yard. He knocked things over. He dug a huge hole in the backyard. When we gave him his food we poured it on his head." Almost as an afterthought Jack added a last line: "He is a pig."

Soon, Jack and Ned were saving their banana peels and corncobs, their leftover pancakes, cupcakes, and Danishes; because the family lived part-time in another home in Cambridge, Massachusetts, they had to freeze it. "We wouldn't buy stuff for ourselves because the freezer was filled with stuff for the pig," Mollie told us. "Our ice cream smelled like corncobs and old pancakes—but we didn't care. We knew how much Christopher would appreciate it." When they'd come up to Hancock, often each boy would bring a friend or two with them, and together we'd do Pig Spa. "It was part of the Hancock tour," Mollie said: "Go see the Elephant Rock. Go to Spoonwood Pond. Do the rope swing on the lake. And go see Christopher."

One day after Pig Spa, Christopher lay in such peaceful bliss that Jack thought to join him. Very gently, and with great respect, Jack climbed on top of him. He lay with his head on Chris's shoulder. Christopher's skin felt like cardboard and his bristles were spiky, but Jack was enchanted. He could hear the pig's breathing. He could feel the beating of his huge heart. "He was really gentle and really nice," Jack said. "It felt really, really good." Next, the boys switched positions and Ned lay down on Christopher.

Remarkably, Christopher didn't object at all. Had he been the least bit uncomfortable, he wouldn't have been shy about showing it. Even Bob, who is far more in tune with people than with animals and who had initially been quite fearful for his kids around this huge beast, could see: "He clearly enjoyed Jack and Ned lying on top of him," Bob said. "He didn't want it to end."

Mollie snapped a picture, and that became our holiday pig card that year.

Time had been good to us: our animals were older but still vigorous. Howard was happily at work on a new book about our oldest landmarks, trees and rocks, and our allegiance to the natural markers that tie us to the land. I had spent part of the fall in French Guiana chasing after quarter-pound goliath bird-eater spiders for a book for kids about tarantulas. Afterward, sometimes I would enjoy happy dreams of tarantulas crawling on me, reliving the feel of their clawlike tarsi on my skin.

Just before I'd left on that expedition, though, I'd made a far more momentous trip: one to Virginia, to see my mother. On and off for the previous two years, I'd traveled with Gary to Cambodia, Thailand, and Laos in search of a mysterious golden bear unknown to science—which we found, among many other adventures. I dedicated the resulting book to my mother, and we celebrated at a local bookstore by a reading and signing attended by all her friends. At that moment, I knew that whatever else had happened between us, she was proud of me. I stayed over at her house for the first time since my father had died.

It seemed a good way to close out the year: everyone I loved was well, and all was right with the world.

Our Christmas card that year bore the message, "Peace."

And then, on a Wednesday afternoon in March, my mother began to die.

We'd known something was wrong for only a couple of months. She'd gotten the bad news on Martin Luther King Jr. Day but didn't phone me. She waited for my usual Sunday after-church call. She went in to her doctor at Fort Belvoir with a stomachache, she said, and came out with pancreatic cancer. The doctors gave her a year.

So began another flurry of flying to and from Virginia. Still, Howard was unwelcome. He stayed in Hancock, working on his next book, and took care of our aging animals. I arranged for some relatively gentle chemo to slow the disease's progress, hired nurses and housekeepers, and cooked and froze piles of collard greens, cornbread, and fried fish.

But the disease kept racing ahead of us. That particular Wednesday was just four days shy of a scheduled move to an elegant new assisted-living facility we had selected, just a few miles from her house. Surprisingly, my mother looked forward to the move; she'd have the best of both worlds. We'd keep the house, and when I'd come back to Virginia, we'd stay there together, where I could take care of her.

We planned on plenty of time together in the months ahead. I could not make her approve of my life, but I could learn more about hers. She could not bring herself to love the man I had married, but I could accept the love she gave me, and love her fully in return. There would be good days, many of them, the doctors told us—and we would spend them talking together, reminiscing, looking through photo albums.

While my father was alive, he dominated our conversations, for both my mother and I adored him and hung on his every word. Now, for the first time in my life, I would learn the details of my mother's youth in Arkansas: how she had learned to shoot a gun and fly a plane, how she was recruited from Arkansas Tech to work for the FBI. I'd learn about the early days of her courtship and marriage to my father. We would go through everything carefully, lovingly—the memories, the jewelry, the heirlooms—and in so doing, at the end of her life, I would finally come to know my elegant, enigmatic mother. We would pack each gem of her life away as gently as the hand-crafted glass ornaments my parents had bought in Germany for year after year of our Christmas trees, and gracefully, gently, say our good-byes.

But we never did.

That Wednesday, when I phoned my mother, as I'd been doing daily since I learned of the cancer, she didn't answer. I got the home nurse, who said they were going to the doctor. Fifteen minutes later, I phoned the doctor, who said they were going to the hospital. Next I phoned the hospital, and they said she was going to die.

I booked the next flight to D.C. I asked Liz to drive me to the airport. I was in the air at seven, at my mother's bedside by ten.

She was on morphine for the pain, but still clear-minded. After about half an hour, she insisted I go back to the house and go to sleep. I was afraid I was keeping her up, draining her energy. I checked with the nurses. "She'll be fine for the night," they said.

But that prediction did not hold true of things back home.

The phone rang at 4 a.m. It was Howard. "Tess is having a stroke!" he said. She had soiled herself, fallen over, vomited, and now couldn't stand. She was panting and agitated. "What should I do?"

I'D BEEN PLAGUED BY NIGHTMARES LIKE THIS WHILE RESEARCHING *Search for the Golden Moon Bear* in Southeast Asia. I'd dream Tess or Chris was sick and I couldn't get to them, and I would wake up screaming.

Gary assured me there was a physical cause for my nightmares. Vivid dreams and even hallucinations were known side effects of the antimalarial drug we were taking. But I thought the real reason was one of the common ailments that shamans in this region are called upon to treat: a dangerous condition known as soul wandering.

According to the hill tribes of northern Thailand—many of them migrants and refugees from another land—the soul is prone to wander, easily enticed away, and apt to flee in fear. Lost souls can fall prey to malevolent spirits, weretigers, and vampires. So the different hill tribes have devised many ways to recapture the wandering or lost soul, and shamans are specially trained in the art of soul calling. The Lahu and Hmong say that even a newborn's soul might flee from loud noises. For this reason, mothers give birth in utter silence, and then embroider their babies' clothes with soul-restraining designs: spiderwebs are one favorite, pigpens another.

Loud noises weren't my problem—although at one point, when we had visited Cambodia, Gary and I did hear a land mine explode from an area where we had just been walking, and it gave us a start. My soul was deeply disturbed by the incongruence of an Edenic-looking tropical rain forest beset with unexploded ordnance, banditry, insurgency, and a sickening trade using wild animals' body parts for medicinal elixirs and tonics. Everywhere, on our trail to scientific discovery, we found horror and sorrow. In Cambodia, 1 in 236 people are amputees. In Laos, we were constantly warned against the dangers of unexploded ordnance from a war in which more bombs were rained on that small country than on Germany in World War II. In Thailand, we even met an elephant who was an amputee. She had stepped on a land mine while her mahout was using her for illegal logging in Burma. My dreams, I thought, were evidence that my soul was desperately, though unsuccessfully, trying to escape the nightmares that these people and animals live daily.

When we visited a Lahu village in northern Thailand, only Gary and I knew about the dreams I'd been having, and yet the shaman seemed to sense them. He offered to perform a healing ceremony. While we sat on woven mats on the floor of the stilt house where he lived, he fetched a bowl of rice, a set of candles, some paper, and a ball of string. He did the same thing to both of us in turn. Holding a thread taut, he wiped one of our palms with it thrice before circling one wrist with it five times, closing the circle firmly with knots.

He was tying our souls to our bodies.

"You travel around, around everywhere," the shaman said to me through our translator, "but in the end, you will come back. Your spirit will always come back."

A calm settled over me at that moment as I felt my soul restored. I realized I was meant to witness both suffering and hope on this journey—and that the strength I was given to do so was derived from a soul firmly bound to home.

AT FOUR THAT MORNING, WITH MY MOTHER ON HER DEATHBED and Tess helpless in New Hampshire, I didn't think things could get worse. My heart was torn in two. There are people who would be appalled at the thought of a daughter fearing for the life of a dog in the face of the death of her own mother. But as I sat by my mother's side the next few days in the hospital, my thoughts were as much with Tess as with my mother.

How could this be? Leaving aside the issue of species, I had known Tess for only twelve years. I had known my mother for forty-five. My mother had given me my life. But I had not chosen the life she had wanted for me—and this was a sin she found very difficult to forgive. Early in life, my mother had learned to make sure she got what she wanted, and it worked: the daughter of an iceman and a postmistress from dusty Lexa went to college, learned to fly a plane, landed a glamorous job in Washington, and married a dashing war hero. I had been the first big disappointment of her life. Though she loved me, her love was conditional—and for most of my life, I met very few of her conditions.

But I was Tess's person. We were a unit. We were family. Because I loved her with almost drunken abandon, and because she loved me so completely and deeply, I believed I might love Tess back to life. I knew I could not do this for my mother. Her person was my father, and he had already passed on to a place she was eager to go. Yet I knew at that moment where I needed to be: in the hospital in Virginia, by my mother's side, where perhaps there was still hope of another kind of healing.

My mother was tired, but glad for company that next day. I slipped out only when other visitors came to see her. I was deeply moved to see how many there were: women from the neighborhood, friends from church, old Army friends, bridge players, members of the Villamay Ladies' Club, women from the sewing circle. At these times I would visit the hall pay phone and call Chuck to check on Tess.

Chuck told me Tess had not had a stroke. Her disorder was called canine peripheral vestibular syndrome. No one knows what causes it, but for whatever reason, the animal is seized with a vertigo so powerful it cannot stand, walk, or eat, because its world is spinning—sometimes for weeks. The trick, Chuck said, was to find a way to get food into her and to keep her from succumbing to some other disease while the vestibular problem dissipated—or her brilliant border collie brain found a way to compensate.

The timing could not have been worse. Howard had to fly

to Pittsburgh that afternoon to give a speech on Friday. Because of Tess's separation anxiety, for the last twelve years we'd made sure she never spent a single night apart from at least one of us except at Evelyn's, where she had lived before coming to us. We had always been with her for every procedure at the vet's, never leaving her for a minute. Now she would have to endure the scariest night of her life alone, locked in a cage in a veterinary hospital, the world swirling inexplicably around her.

Tess was terrified, but my mother was neither sad nor frightened. Dying did not bother her at all. We had spoken of this a little in the weeks before. For her, death was the portal to my father. She was eager to see him in heaven. Only one thing bothered her: she was worried, incredibly, that my father might not be there.

"Of course he is!" I cried, appalled. Who deserved heaven if not my father? "If my father's not there," I said, "heaven is full of idiots, and I'm not going."

My outburst did not calm my mother. Her worry was this: although my father's religion was listed on his dog tags as Roman Catholic, she was not sure, she told me, that he *really believed in Jesus*. Heaven, she feared, excluded those who did not—condemning my Hindu friends in West Bengal, my Buddhist friends in Southeast Asia, most of my scientific colleagues (who were atheist or agnostic), Liz (a believer in Gaia), Gretchen (an animist), Selinda (an atheist), my in-laws, and my husband.

At that moment I deeply regretted ever having told my mother about a phone call I had received before she got sick. A cousin I'd never known I had—a daughter of my father's vanished brother, who had died before my birth—had read a review of one of my books and found my phone number on the

Internet. At first I was unsure that we were related at all. But as she told me details of my father's family history, I knew everything she said was true—as well as wildly different from what I had earlier been told.

My father's ancestry was not Scottish and English, as I had believed. My father's grandfather, an opera star, was from Italy. His name had been Montegriffo. His son, my grandfather, born in this country with blond hair and blue eyes, had changed it to Montgomery. Brilliant, ambitious, and blessed with total auditory recall, when he graduated from law school my grandfather had been courted by many law firms. But Italians were not then slated to become lawyers in America. What did Italians do? I remembered a little ditty my father would sometimes utter in my childhood, along with snippets of Ogden Nash and Lewis Carroll: "Guinea, Guinea goo / Shine my shoe." I didn't realize until many years later that *guinea* was slang for Italian, nor that this little rhyme described why my brilliant grandfather kept his heritage—and my father's— hidden for the rest of their lives.

My father's mother was also a lawyer—a fact that I had been proud of growing up. That was all I had known of her, that and the single six-inch-tall photo that sat in its oval golden frame on a desk in a spare bedroom. She was an elegant and pretty brunette, wearing pearls and lace and a feathered hat. I had always been told her name was Augusta Black. Her name, my cousin told me, was, in fact, Augusta *Schwartz*. I recognized the word: it was Yiddish for "black." My cousin told me that my grandmother's parents had emigrated to the United States from Austria, fleeing religious persecution. She was Jewish. Her law degree had been financed by B'nai B'rith. Of course when she married my grandfather, she had acquired his rewritten, Americanized name, and all outward evidence of her heritage disappeared. But that didn't change Jewish law—nor the tradition that any children born to a Jewish mother, no matter who the father, are Jewish, too.

When I had told my mother these things, there had been a long silence. I realized I never should have mentioned this. It was miracle enough that my mother and I could love each other at all, after everything that had happened; nothing would ever make her accept my husband. I certainly did not wish to undermine her love of hers. My mother confirmed that yes, the woman who had called me was indeed my cousin—but she must have gotten her story wrong. She changed the subject, and we never brought it up again.

Only after my mother's death did I learn, from an old family friend in whom my father had once confided, how fiercely my father had guarded his secret: while my father lived, my mother had never known that her husband, like mine, was Jewish.

The doctors were frank: there was nothing they could do for my mother but turn up the morphine. So I slept beside her each night, holding her hand. Once she brought my hand to her mouth and kissed it. After this, she no longer spoke. She no longer needed to say anything. I spoke very little: "I love you, Mother. I'm here, Mother." That was all. And it was enough.

During those days, I came to know some of the eclectic friends who had peopled her weekly letters, folks I had only met briefly. Of course I already knew some friends from when I'd lived in Virginia in junior high: the neighbors next door, whose son and daughter I used to babysit for twenty-five cents an hour. The folks whose backyard abutted ours, whose daughter had shown me the local creek and how to find box turtles there. My mother also had many friends from the military, especially from the Army's Transportation Corps. But in the years since my father died, my mother had made new, young friends as well: Scott Marchard, originally from my mother's home state of Arkansas, a dapper florist in his forties with a single earring, sat next to my mother in church. In the hospital, the nurses assumed he was her son. Silver Crossman, a fit, witty, single woman a little older than me, with a beloved puppy named Summer. For years, my mother had called Silver "daughter number two." In her isolated widowhood, my mother, like me, had surrounded herself with an alternative family.

Meanwhile, when I was in Virginia, my alternative family did for me what relatives are supposed to do: they took care of my loved ones in my absence. When Howard was in Pittsburgh, Gretchen and Liz visited Tess in the animal hospital. Liz went to the house first and picked up my barn coat. She placed it beside Tess in her hospital cage so she could inhale my scent. Immediately, Liz told me, Tess's ears relaxed, her face assumed a peaceful expression, she uttered a sigh, and she shut her eyes.

Jarvis and Bobbie and our new tenant looked after Christopher and the hens. And when Howard came back to find a March thaw flooding the chicken coop with snowmelt, Selinda's husband, Ken, came with a sump pump—Howard couldn't leave Tess alone in the house long enough to buy one. To tempt Tess to eat, Selinda brought her homemade meatballs; Gretchen brought ground raw venison.

Back in the hospital room, as my mother's life faded, her friends came and went: The pastors from the Methodist church. A retired WAVE nurse from Bethesda—she had met my father long before he knew my mother, when he was testifying at the war crimes trials in Japan. On Sunday morning, Silver and Scott came by. And that was when she died—

surrounded by friends, free of pain and fear. I was holding her hand.

EACH CHRISTMAS SINCE MY FATHER DIED, MY MOTHER USED TO invite me to come "home" for the holiday in Virginia. Of course she never invited Howard. So I never came.

Christmas meant nothing to Howard, but it was important to me. We had a holiday ritual. Chris would have a special breakfast. I'd make hot popcorn for the hens. Tess would come with us as we drove to our friends' houses to exchange gifts and visit: sometimes to Liz and Steve's, sometimes to Eleanor's, sometimes to Gretchen's. Always, though, I wanted to begin Christmas Day much as Jesus had—in a barn.

But the Christmas after my mother died was different.

That morning, after I'd given Hogwood his holiday slops, I was bringing the Ladies a bowl of hot popcorn when I found a hen dead on the coop floor. Her head was wedged down a hole in a corner. Whoever had killed her had dug its way in. I bent over to pick her up by her feet—and found that someone else had a hold of the other end of the chicken!

I pulled her carcass free. And then, out of the hole in the corner popped a tiny, pure white head. It stared at me with fearless black eyes. It was an ermine.

Ermine is the name by which we call both of our tiny New Hampshire weasel species when they're dressed in their white winter coats. I had never seen one before. They are only a few inches long, and exactly the color of snow.

Without backing down, the ermine looked at me, square in the eye, for perhaps thirty seconds. I had never seen a gaze so exquisitely fierce, so intense, so filled with the moment. Ermines may weigh as little as five ounces, less than a handful of coins, yet they are as fearless as God. They stop at nothing to capture their prey: they snake down tunnels, they hunt beneath the snow, they will even leap into the air to catch birds as they take flight. With their tiny hearts pounding 360 times a minute, ermines must eat five to ten meals a day. They are fierce because they have to be. This is part of what makes ermines what they are. Ferocity is their dharma—as pure, and as perfect, as their dazzling white winter coat.

The ermine had just killed someone I loved. Yet I could not have felt more amazed, or more blessed, if an angel had materialized in front of me.

My sorrow vanished. Holding the still-warm body of my hen in my arms, I felt, in that moment, the lightness of a heart relieved of the burden of anger—and the freedom that comes with forgiveness.

CHAPTER 12

COMING BACK TO LIFE

IN YOUNGER DAYS, AFTER WE'D CLOSE CHRIS IN FOR THE EVENING, right before we would go upstairs to bed, Tess, Howard, and I would always play a final round of Frisbee in the yard. On full-moon nights, Tess had looked so beautiful: her sleek black and white form flying over the field like a spirit, leaping to catch the toy in her jaws, then racing back to us, gilded in moonlight.

But she was even more beautiful on inky, moonless nights, when we couldn't see her at all. Of course, back then, Tess could see perfectly in the dark. The tapetum lucidum—the light-gathering reflector in the eye that makes dogs' eyes glow when they catch the light at night—guided her through the blackness, the heritage of a predator who hunted both day and night. Humans, like pigs, lack such night vision. But we can enjoy the next best thing: the company of a dog.

Howard and I would follow Tess into the night, listening to the jingle of her tags, down to where the lawn leveled out to the field. Then we would whisper: "Tess—go!" and toss the Frisbee into the darkness. A second or two later, we would hear the dramatic click of her teeth on the plastic and know Tess had leaped into the air and caught it. The scene was all the more beautiful for the fact it was invisible. It was our private little miracle: each time she brought us the Frisbee, she gave us the gift of navigating through the dark.

With the events of March, we had left those days behind. Never again did Tess play Frisbee with us. It was weeks before she could even walk. She had the heart of a lion. The same way my dying father had struggled for that last, delicious breath of air, Tess—deaf, wobbly, and now nearly blind—had fought for a life she still found full of joy and meaning, rich with scent, full of tasty treats, and secure in the company of those she most loved.

By the time the wood frog chorus swelled in April, Tess was strong enough to walk outside with us again. Now she would stay close by, following our heat and scent. I remembered the lost magic of her younger nights, how she'd leap through the dark to catch the unseen Frisbee. But then I realized she had not lost that gift; she had simply brought it back to us, like the Frisbee. Now it was our turn; now we would lead her through the darkness.

There would be much darkness in the months ahead. Often—too often—despite medicine and prayer, despite faith and strength, the ones we love are torn from us, sometimes viciously, for reasons no one can fathom. But sometimes God, or luck, or the universe itself allows you a rare opportunity. That is the gift that the darkness brought: the knowledge that sometimes you really can love someone back to life.

Pig visitors that summer got quite a different show from years previous: as we left the house, out would stumble a fifteen-year-old deaf and mostly blind border collie, holding her head at a forty-five-degree tilt. Sometimes I'd carry Tess partway to the barnyard, where we'd be greeted by a flock of hens composed partly of menopausal birds so aged that some of them had grown spurs on their feet like a rooster. Then, armed with the most tempting of slops, we would coax the arthritic Chris to limp from his pen. Sometimes he just couldn't be bothered to step over the threshold, knowing that usually he could just stay in the nice, cool barn—which Howard had recently upgraded by installing a rotating fan—while a crowd of admirers gratefully placed pastries in his open mouth.

But Christopher still knew how to rally for the right audience. When the *Chronicle* sent a TV team back to our barn to film a short retrospective on our pig that May, Chris played expertly to the camera. Christopher looked the lens in the eye, grunted forthrightly, then stepped out of his pen smartly as the camera rolled. "Oh, this is *great!*" the host cried as Chris ate blueberry muffins from my hand. "He's the only one on the block who's not on Atkins," I said—and Christopher grunted in agreement, as if on cue. The moment they had enough footage of the pig eating, Christopher lay down on request. The cameraman shot several minutes of Christopher lying luxuriously in the sun, flicking away blackflies with his lavishly furred ears and flexing his moist nose disk exactly like an expert fashion model on the runway. Well, maybe not *exactly*—but as close as it gets around here.

When children came for Pig Spa, Christopher would almost always rise to the occasion. One afternoon the Miller-Rodats came with Jack and Ned and a friend, Isabel. Christopher displayed his entire repertoire: He trotted to the Plateau. He devoured slops greedily. He dug an enormous hole with his snout that the kids pronounced "like, so *awesome!*" We rubbed his belly and he lay down and allowed us to wash him with sponges and massage him with aloe-scented skin cream.

After a luxurious hour or so, it was time for Chris to go back in his pen. Howard was again off premises, and I would soon have to clean up and leave for a slide lecture I was giving at a local library.

But Christopher wouldn't get up.

Why should he? He was perfectly happy where he was. He was lying in the sunshine being petted by adoring children. If he got up, he knew full well that he'd be leaving the sun for his pen, and the children and I would go away. Why should he leave all this behind? Nothing doing. He was no fool.

Fortunately I had considered this possibility and brought a box of a dozen chocolate doughnuts to help lure him back to the pen. What I had not factored in was that during Pig Spa, the children would eat some of them.

We lured Chris to his feet with a first doughnut. A second doughnut got him moving forward. He stood there chewing it with a thoughtful look on his face. We knew he was considering turning back to the Plateau—or possibly strolling out to the pasture. We gave him another doughnut in an attempt to dissuade such thinking. Christopher walked forward several paces and then opened his cavernous mouth. He wanted another doughnut. We popped one in. A few more paces. His mouth opened again, his lips shaking with anticipation.

But now, disaster—we were out of doughnuts! Christopher dug another "awesome" hole with his nose, and halfway between the Plateau and his pen, he lay down. It was the worst possible scenario: now he was completely loose without even a tether to hold him, and I, still dressed for Pig Spa, had thirty-five minutes to get to a formal slide presentation at a library that was a half-hour's drive away.

We dispatched Mollie to the Cash Market to buy more doughnuts.

I made it to the library about ten minutes late. I was forgiven when I explained that I had been waylaid by a recalcitrant pig. The audience, many of them children, knew about Chris already, because the librarian—the wife of our optometrist—was on our Christmas mailing list and had been vamping for time recounting Chris's adventures.

THE TROUBLE IN THE NEXT YEAR BEGAN WITH A BUCKET OF SLOPS. We always checked Chris's slops bucket, for a number of excellent reasons. The first was to satisfy our curiosity, as there was local culinary history in those slops buckets. Oops, somebody burned the brownies again. And who overestimated the pancake batter? Well, *that* soup didn't go over. We could also look into the slops bucket and foretell the future. Were there lots of melon rinds? Remains of hors d'oeuvre rollups? That was evidence of a catered event—often one we might well attend ourselves. Our pig's cuisine would give us a peek at the party menu.

We also scanned the slops with safety in mind. Although Fiddleheads' employees were generally very careful, occasionally someone would forget and toss a napkin, a plastic bag, or a toothpick into the bucket for Hogwood's slops. Also, we wanted to make sure nothing had spoiled.

And finally, there was simply the matter of balance. Sometimes we would get a bucket of mostly one thing. Pigs are not known for their innate sense of moderation, so if we got an entire bucket of mainly, say, hash brown potatoes, we would try to administer it in smaller doses. You never want to give anyone too much of a good thing.

But sometimes the slops seemed to have a mind of their own. Especially when the buckets were heavy with slippery items, the slops would plop out in one big bolus, and Christopher would have a bonanza. And that is what happened one bitterly cold January morning, when I tipped the bucket toward Chris's bowl and out slid about five gallons of tomato sauce.

Chris slurped happily. His appetite was excellent, and no wonder: this was one of those brutally cold days when a trace of moisture on your hands will cause your skin to freeze to a metal doorknob, and the hairs in your nose will freeze as stiff as a porcupine's quills. Even with all that lard and his fluffy bed of fresh hay, Chris needed extra calories to stay warm. Maybe all that tomato sauce was a good thing: I recalled having read recently about the medicinal wonders of tomatoes—the cancer-fighting carotenes, the lycopene for eye health—and I didn't worry.

Until a few hours later, when I returned to find Chris lying on his side and moaning.

He had suffered tummy aches before. (More of them than I had realized: Howard had spent more than a few nights up beside the pig while I had been in Southeast Asia, as Chris recovered from indigestion.) In fact, Chris had suffered a bout of digestive trouble just before Christmas, but after a meal of warm bran mash, which I sweetened with molasses and fed him with a spoon, he was fine again.

So this was what I tried that evening. He ate a few spoonfuls, and drank some warm water I poured into his mouth from a yogurt cup.

But in the morning, he was worse. He didn't stand to eat.

He lay on his side. His grunts were weak. Even more upsetting, he would take a breath, hold it, and then let it go in a shivering moan. Worse yet, he felt cold to my touch. I had never seen anyone who looked this sick who survived. I was terrified and called Chuck at home.

Chuck said it was the tomato sauce. "Tomatoes are no good for pigs!" he told me. In all my fourteen years of swineherding, I had never known.

"What's wrong with tomatoes?" I asked.

"Too acidic," he replied.

The solution? Try to get him to swallow some activated charcoal—I actually had a huge bottle of this, left over from a digestive ailment I had acquired in Southeast Asia—and get some antacids into him. How many? "As many as you can get him to eat."

This was easier said than done. I was faced with an unusual problem: Christopher did not want to open his mouth.

As Howard reminded me of the variable quality of our small local hospital's emergency room, I forced my freezing, naked fingers past the thicket of Chris's tusks and teeth.

First I placed the antacid into the cavern of his mouth, tiny pills that I thought he would surely swallow. A few went in, but then what? I don't know that he ever knew they were there. Did he swallow them? It didn't look like it to me.

"Come on, sweetie," I begged. "Please eat this for me."

"Unh." Nothing doing.

"Please!"

"Unnnnnnnn!" He was getting irritated.

Next I tried Tums. Because these were larger and sweet like candy, I hoped they might prove more promising. He spat them out. I tossed in activated charcoal capsules—but because they are black, I couldn't tell whether they simply fell out the other side of his mouth or not. I poured in a bottle of Pepto-Bismol. The pink liquid oozed out his lips.

There was nothing to do but stay with him. In the eleven-below-zero weather, I put one arm around him and lay down beside him in the hay. Howard came out and brought us a blanket.

IT SEEMED CHRISTOPHER FELT BETTER THE NEXT DAY, BUT HE still wouldn't eat. He wouldn't open his mouth for warm mash, not even sweetened with molasses. I couldn't tempt him with the choicest slops. I made him soup. He wouldn't touch it. When he spat out a pastry, I burst into tears. The tears froze to my face.

But he would drink warm water. When I poured it into his mouth, he opened wide for more. Later that day he stood up for a shaky moment as I poured water into his dish. Chuck came out and decided Chris needed injections of a really powerful antacid. To my horror, he gave me a needle three inches long, mounted on a syringe so big the entire assembly looked like the Empire State Building—so huge I almost couldn't look at it. But that's what we needed to get past all that lard and inject ten cubic centimeters—about two teaspoons—of antacid into Christopher's backside, twice a day.

Howard wouldn't even watch.

I carefully chose my plan of attack. I would administer these shots when Chris was lying down, I decided, with his back end facing the gate—my exit, in case I had to make a speedy one. I would pet and scratch his back end for a time before giving the injection. And right before the jab, I would smack the site smartly with my knuckle twice—a trick I remembered a humane nurse using on me during one of many series of shots I had needed for my travels, and which I had thought considerably dulled the pain of the injection.

But nothing I could do could have prevented Christopher from disliking my jabbing a three-inch needle deep into his flesh. He had every right to bite me. He never did. True, he said some horrible things to me—his emphatic grumbles and occasional roars could have been the sound track to a monster movie—but I knew he didn't mean it. When the shot was over I would crawl under the blanket and lie down beside him in the hay, and he would push his back up against me and give love grunts as I rubbed his belly.

Days went by, and still he wouldn't eat more than a spoonful or two of mash. He didn't want bagels. He didn't want bread. He neglected his pastries. Squirrels who retrieved the uneaten treats from his dish tried, unsuccessfully, to pull them through holes in the barn's stone foundation, to hide them in tunnels. As a result, I would find bagels and muffins lodged in the holes in the wall at odd angles, like some weird installation from the Museum of Modern Art in New York.

Chris's breathing sounded wet, so Chuck came by and gave him a shot of antibiotics. We switched drugs: a mix of two powerful antibiotics, plus Banamine, a strong painkiller. Finally Christopher turned the corner: no sooner had I given him his shot than he stood up, wheeled around, and growl-grunted, "Nynhunnnnnr!"—enough already!

I phoned Liz with the daily pig update to give her the good news. After my torrent of veterinary details, I asked, finally, "And how are you?"

Came the reply: "I have cancer."

Liz does not complain. The mastectomy, she insisted, would be nothing more than "a haircut." She insisted that her daughter, Stephie, not bother to come from Texas. Her son, Ramsay, was mountain-guiding in France, and his wife, Heather, was pregnant with their first child—of course Liz insisted they stay there. Liz sent her husband, Steve, back to Prague, where he had been researching a book on nationalism, to continue his work. So I didn't ask her if I could go with her for the operation; I announced it.

We were still awaiting Liz's surgery date when I called to say hello on February 6. The next day would be my forty-sixth birthday. With Chris on the mend and Tess stable, I was going to join a host of friends and colleagues at the annual meeting of the International Bear Association in San Diego. The hotel had a sea lion living on the premises.

"Hi, Liz—how are you?"

She hesitated, and my blood froze.

Ramsay had been in an accident.

While mountain-guiding on a ski slope at the Swiss-French border, he had fallen and hit his head earlier that morning. He was in a coma. The brain damage was severe, the doctors said. He might die. He might never come out of the coma. He might live to be a human vegetable. Or he might be dead even now. Liz's only source of information was his wife, Heather, alone in a foreign country with her comatose husband, seven months pregnant with their first child, and struggling to understand the doctors' French.

I announced, "I'm coming over."

The next day, together, we flew to Geneva.

TOGETHER WE FACED THE LONG, STRANGE, ELASTIC HOSPITAL hours, the sleepless hotel nights, the frantic phone calls home at weird hours. Day after day, together we offered our eager, loving presence to Ramsay and to Heather. The word *compas-*

sion means "with suffering." To have compassion is to willingly join in suffering—to show those you love that you will not let them suffer alone. And this is the most you can do: offer your presence.

One beautiful day, Ramsay opened an eye. It was as unexpected, as miraculous, as blessed as witnessing the opening eye of the Hindu Creator, Vishnu, who slumbers on the coils of the endless serpent, Ananta, on the sea of eternity. And then, days later, he opened the other eye. None of the surgeons, none of the doctors, none of the nurses or therapists or aides dared voice even the possibility of what was happening, but I had seen it before: Ramsay, like Tess and Chris, was coming back to us.

I flew home first, and Liz followed a few days later. Steve stayed with Heather and Ramsay. Stephie flew to New Hampshire from Texas so we both could be by Liz's side for the mastectomy. The surgery, though gruesome, was a success. The cancer was gone.

We began to make plans for Ramsay and Heather to come home to New Hampshire. Ramsay would start rehab, to get his strength back; Heather would bear their child. Spring was just around the corner.

SPRING IS A FARRIER'S BUSIEST SEASON, BUT STILL, GEORGE MADE time to come and trim Christopher's hooves.

Mary hadn't even told him I'd phoned until days after my call. She wasn't thrilled about her husband messing with the feet of a seven-hundred-pound pig. Chris had never had his hooves trimmed before. Even horses who regularly require a farrier's services don't like it; for one thing, they don't like standing on three hooves while a person cuts off pieces of the fourth. They usually take out their displeasure on the farrier.

And, understandably, perhaps Mary didn't really want George to postpone good, paying work to risk his life servicing a "customer" from whom he'd never accept a cent.

But Chris really needed him. In Christopher's younger days, his hooves had been trimmed naturally by his frequent walks. But in the past year, because of his arthritis, they had grown long and awkward. The longer they grew, the more uncomfortable his feet became—and the less likely he was to walk at all.

So I was surprised and delighted when George appeared at the door a couple of days later. "I just found out about your call from Mary," George apologized, "and I came as soon as I could!"

We went out to the pen, and Christopher grunted a greeting. He did not stand up. This made things easier for George, and he appreciated it as much as if Chris had done him a conscious favor—and perhaps he had. Surely it was easier on Chris not to have to balance on three legs while having his trim. While I stroked his belly, Christopher didn't wiggle or thrash. He let George go about his work quietly and efficiently.

George had only visited a couple of times before, and each time he saw Chris he would praise his size, his condition, his attitude. I was always happy to hear this, and reminded him that he and Mary had made this all possible. "Where there's life, there's hope," George used to say. He had given us both all those years ago, with the gift of a sickly runt at a time when I thought I would lose everything.

And now, as he trimmed the big old pig's overgrown hooves, George had something new to say about Christopher.

"This pig," he said sincerely, "has been so *successful*!"

I was deeply moved by his choice of words. In the vocabulary of a yuppie, *success* can be a nasty word, the sort of thing that makes you jealous when you read your alumni magazine. But when a hippie farmer calls someone successful, it is stripped of the clutch and shove of money, power, and ego, and achieves a more important meaning. And when the word *success* is applied to a pig, we get to its most fundamental meaning: success is achieved by escaping the freezer. Christopher Hogwood had outlived everyone in his class by thirteen and a half years.

Even on a human playing field, Christopher Hogwood's life would have been considered a success by many measures. Many people would consider their lives a success to attain just a fraction of Christopher's fame. But I knew that George meant something else.

Christopher's success was fourteen years of comfort and joy, given and received. Christopher was a gift who kept on giving. For me, his greatest gift was simply his presence, the pure delight of his company. But he had given me so much more: He had introduced me to my neighbors. He had helped me overcome my shyness with people. He had showed me how to play with children. He had even brought me a garden. And his success didn't end with us. This huge, adored pig, who had given so many people delight, was proof that no matter what nature or history hands you, with love, anything is possible.

And now, with spring soon to flower, I was grateful.

Soon there would be tulips, and then lilacs, and then strawberries. Feeling loved and lucky, I stood on the tender lip of spring, open to the healing summer.

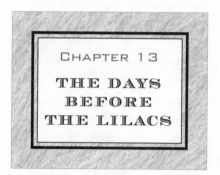

CHAPTER 13

THE DAYS
BEFORE
THE LILACS

THAT FRIDAY WAS A BEAUTIFUL MAY DAY—THE TREES AT LAST lush with leaves, the grass as emerald as a rice field. Our crab apple and quince were a mass of hot pink and salmon petals, heavy with bumblebees. In a day or two, the apple trees in the field would come into bloom, and soon thereafter, the lilacs I love would flower, arching over our doorway, filling the whole world with their scent.

On a day like this, of course, Chris would want to be outside. So shortly before noon, although we were out of slops, I tried to lure him to the Pig Plateau with grain.

Although he stepped over the threshold with relative ease, he wasn't particularly interested in the grain. He had taken only perhaps thirty paces out of his pen when he made his decision: he had now arrived at the spot where he wanted to root with his nose, expose the cool, damp, fragrant earth, and lie down in the sun. There was nothing I could do.

You try to be mad at a pig at a time like that. I needed to go inside and get to work. And the blackflies were swarming—which didn't bother Christopher but really bothered me. "Terrible!" I said. "You're being a terrible animal! A dreadful beast!" But, of course, I said this as I bent over to stroke his ear, and then leaned in to pat his belly—and next I found myself kneeling in the freshly dug earth, rubbing the length of his stomach. He grunted in a cadence that said ha-ha-ha, as if he was laughing at the joke he had played on me once again.

I couldn't blame him, of course. Why should he walk the additional yards down to the Pig Plateau when things looked so inviting here? For him, as always, the immediate fulfillment of pleasure was utterly, unquestionably paramount. His priorities were always clear.

So he laid his huge body down in the dirt. And once again, swatting at blackflies, I was powerless before the great, swelling tide of Christopher's desires.

Ah, but there *was* one thing we could do: we could appeal to Chris's Higher Power.

I dispatched Howard to go get fresh slops.

Fiddleheads came through, providing three buckets, one of which featured doughnuts floating in a sea of pancake batter. As Howard retreated from the flies, I fished out one of the doughnuts and dropped it inches from Christopher's head.

The pig stretched his huge head forward and tried to lengthen his lips to bring the doughnut to his mouth. He couldn't. Getting the doughnut would require standing. And with the sun so warm, the earth moist and cool . . . well, after all, he wasn't starving.

But then a hen came to my rescue. Spotting the doughnut,

she raced over, eyed it with surgical precision, and began to peck at it, enlarging the hole. Another hen saw the prize and joined in. In minutes, everyone in the barnyard would see the bonanza and come running. This was too much for Christopher. He rocked his bulk up sideways, pulled his feet beneath him, uttered a grunt of disapproval, and stood to eat the remains of the doughnut. I was able to entice him down to the Plateau with the remains of the slops. I poured out half, and, with his entourage of pecking chickens, he gorged until he was ready to lie down again in the sun.

Unfortunately, he was still enjoying the sun at 6:15 and was utterly uninterested in coming inside. This was a problem. That evening we were planning to meet Liz's daughter, Stephie, for dinner at 6:30. It was Howard's and my first outing together for any length of time since Tess had become so frail, and Stephanie's first without her family since she'd come from Texas to help with her brother's rehab and the new baby.

We all very much wanted to get together. Because of Tess's condition, we didn't want to leave her, but the single step to our front door made our house inaccessible to Stephie's wheelchair. So we had decided to meet at the Hancock Inn, just a mile away from our house. One of us could drive back and check on Tess during dinner. We really didn't want to drive off and leave our pig out, either—but it was clear, after my many unsuccessful efforts to rouse him, that this was what we would have to do.

We had a lovely supper. After we finished our entrees, Howard went off to check on Tess and Chris while Stephie and I sipped tea. Howard returned looking concerned.

"What's wrong?" I was scared.

"Our dog is OK," Howard reported. "But Chris is lying in a strange position." He was lying as he often did, on the downward slope of the Plateau—but with his legs facing *up*slope.

"Is he upset about this?" I asked.

"No—but there is no way he can get up from that position," Howard answered.

I looked at Stephie for help. She is in line with her mother and Gretchen for the award for Most Supremely Competent Person on Earth. And in this case she was particularly qualified. As a disability rights activist, she might have some advice on how to help an arthritic pig rise to his feet.

In fact, she did. "You need a Hoyer lift. It's not made for pigs," she stated, almost apologetically. "It's for people who can't get out of bed. But it might work for Chris. There are some really big people out there now." She paused.

"Do you have one?" I asked.

"I bet you could order one on the Internet," she said. "It won't do you any good tonight, though."

(Note to self: order Hoyer lift. Do not mention to salesperson it's for a fat, arthritic pig.)

Stephie wanted to come with us and help get Chris up. But considering the steep, dirt slope and the coming darkness, we all pictured what might happen and decided against it. Stephie promised to alert the family when she got back from dinner. If we needed them, she said, just call. Everyone—Ramsay, recovering from his brain injury, Heather, less than two weeks after giving birth, Liz, mostly healed from her surgery, and Steve—all of them would be standing by to help our pig.

Howard and I raced home, hoping that Christopher might have somehow changed position on his own. He hadn't.

"Christopher, how are you, sweetie?" I asked him.

He grunted softly. He was not in the least upset.

"Chris, come on, fat man. Get up," said Howard.

Christopher wouldn't move.

No slops would rouse him. We pulled at his harness to

urge him up, but he seemed to realize he couldn't rise from this position. Yet he was strangely serene. He seemed confident that Howard and I would come up with a solution. He was content to lie there and wait until we did.

Howard and I discussed our options.

"Should we roll him?"

"He's not going to like that."

"What if we tried to move his hindquarters so they were facing downhill? Then he would have his powerful back legs in position to rise."

"I think he's too heavy. I'm also afraid of pulling his legs and hurting him."

"If we roll him, he might keep rolling."

"And right downhill is a giant pricker bush."

"A seven-hundred-pound pig stuck in a pricker bush—at night."

"This isn't good."

"This is terrible."

"You are a terrible beast!" I scolded the recumbent pig. "But we're going to help you. We love you so much."

We couldn't get his hindquarters in position, so we decided to roll him. This required that the pig be completely upside down for a second, with his legs sticking straight up in the air—a position we were sure would not make him happy. He might thrash. He might scream. He might bite. But there was no other option. I took his front legs and Howard took the back.

"One . . . two . . . three!"

He rolled over and hit with one air-expelling grunt. Then he kept sliding—long enough for us to wonder when he'd stop. But once he did, he got up calmly, as if nothing unusual had happened at all. After frowsting in the grass for a bit, and then stopping to scratch his head on the back wall of the writing studio, he followed Howard and me and the slops bucket, meandering slowly, and with dignity, back to his pen.

THE SUNNY WEATHER DIDN'T HOLD FOR THE WEEKEND. CHRIS stayed in his pen Saturday, as it was clouded over and a little windy. On Sunday, the day I was to receive an honorary doctorate of letters from Keene State College, it was raining. I processed to the outdoor stage damply, along with the college president, trustees, and the rest of the platform party who would address the graduates and their families.

The sun began to peek out during the actual ceremony. Howard had to stay with Tess, so Liz, Selinda, Gretchen, and Gretchen's new husband, Peter—a horse trainer turned mortician that she had met at an equine event—were my guests.

"I wish my parents were alive," I began my address, "but today I am surrounded by a significant portion of the people I love most in the world—as are you. So it seems an appropriate moment to talk about blessings."

Indeed, in reading the citation conferring my honorary degree, the robed college trustee had recounted into the microphone some of the unique blessings that I had enjoyed in the past fourteen years of my odd career: "On assignment, you have been chased by an angry gorilla, hunted by a tiger, bitten by a vampire bat, and undressed by an orangutan . . ."

And in my speech, I recounted yet more blessings. I told about my first trip to India, when I was working on *Spell of the Tiger*. My translator, speedboat, scientist, and guide had all fallen through, and I was stuck for a month in a mangrove swamp full of man-eating tigers; my language-tape Bengali was my only means of communication. That was when I had hired Girindra—and acquired a Bengali brother I'd never known I had. I recalled my very first book, *Walking with the Great Apes,* written about my heroines, Jane Goodall, Dian Fossey, and Biruté Galdikas. On my final expedition to Africa to research it—a trip that had been repeatedly rescheduled to fit Jane's busy schedule—Jane, my childhood icon, had broken my heart. I had arrived at Tanzania's Gombe Stream Reserve to find that she had stood me up, leaving me alone with one African research assistant, no food, and the chimps. Instead of chasing Jane, I tracked the chimps myself.

Blessings, all. In each case, I hadn't found what I had hoped for or expected. Instead, I'd discovered something far more exciting or profound—an unexpected insight, a surprise gift. "And that's a pretty good working definition of a blessing," I said. "So go out into the world where your heart calls you. The blessings will come, I promise you that."

I had never made a promise so public. This was the largest audience I had ever addressed: six thousand people. But I was certain this was the deepest truth I knew. "I wish for you the insight to recognize the blessings as such," I said, "and sometimes this is hard. But you'll know it's a blessing if you are enriched and transformed by the experience. So be ready. There are great souls and teachers everywhere. It is your job to recognize them."

As Liz drove me home, I felt awash in joy. Radiant with the love and pride of my dearest friends, I carried home a bouquet of tulips, hyacinths, and daffodils from Selinda's garden, in a vase she had thrown herself at her pottery class. I came home to a house full of flowers. Howard had stepped out briefly to visit artist friends who were great gardeners and come back with armloads of gigantic parrot tulips, the kind with splayed, fringed petals, like flamboyant kisses. I hugged Howard and petted Tess and went out to the barn to see Christopher.

He was cheerful, standing, and eager to come out. Even though it was 5:00, when I opened the gate to go in to pet him, he thrust his big head out and stepped eagerly over the threshold. We walked together to the Plateau. He enjoyed half a bucket of slops—featuring noodles, croissants, strawberries, and some sort of creamy sauce—and he stayed outside until the light began to fade. He was already on his feet when I came to let him in, and he walked back to his pen hardly limping at all. I was thrilled to see him looking so robust. And when he came in, I poured more delicious slops into his bowl, and he was grateful for them, grunting with happiness as he picked out the strawberries first.

More slops were on the way. That night, as I was washing dishes, I heard something fossicking in the slops buckets on the back porch. I opened the door hoping to see a raccoon. Instead, it was Mollie and Bob, who had stopped over on their way back to their other home in Cambridge. They were not raiding the slops buckets but adding to them, decanting a cornucopia of stale baked goods that Ned and Jack had been saving for Chris for the past month or so in their freezer. I noted this was a particularly fine selection, including loaves of French bread, frozen waffles, and chocolate cupcakes with green icing.

After dark, once I closed the chickens in, I slid the barn door shut to Chris's pen as always. "Goodnight, my good, good pig. I love you." And he grunted his goodnight grunt.

I FOUND HIM IN THE MORNING LYING IN HIS USUAL COMFORTABLE position, on his side, trotters outstretched. His eyes were shut, his face peaceful. But I knew right away something was terribly wrong. His stomach was hideously bloated. Probably quite some time earlier, certainly before midnight, Christopher had died in his sleep.

I threw myself upon his great, prone body, as I had done with so many other sorrows before. "No, no, no!" I cried. "How can this be? I love you!"

It seemed impossible. "Wait," Howard said. Looking upon Chris's body, Howard thought surely he would draw another breath. But none came.

We knew that, on a warm day like this one, we could not let his body rest in his stall for long. We would have to bury him right away.

Howard called Bud Adams, whose backhoe attends the funerals of nearly all the large animals in town. He was in the driveway twenty minutes later. Meanwhile, I called Gretchen, Liz, and Selinda. Each one said the same thing, immediately and without question.

"I'm coming—I'll be there as soon as I can."

CHAPTER 14

HOG
HEAVEN

"THIS LETTER IS AN OBITUARY FOR AN ANIMAL," LIZ WROTE TO the newspapers' editors, "a pig named Christopher Hogwood, who died in his sleep on May 9, at age fourteen, in Hancock. From the time he entered their home as an infant until the day of his death last Sunday, he was the beloved companion of Howard Mansfield and Sy Montgomery. We seldom honor animals by noticing their deaths, and the obituary pages, of course, are closed to them. Nevertheless, their passing can leave large holes in our lives—we mourn for them as we mourn for the human members of our family, although our mourning is not acknowledged.

"Christopher was well known, not just in Hancock but throughout New England, as the result of his appearances on various television programs. When a local storekeeper was reluctant to accept my check drawn on an out-of-state bank, he changed his mind and took the check when I named Christopher Hogwood as a reference. Yet it was Christopher's persona, not his fame, that makes his death so saddening. Pigs get bigger as they get older—Christopher must have weighed about 750 pounds. Yet he was discriminating, totally the opposite of the stereotype of his species. It was a pleasure to watch him delicately lift a single strawberry or small cookie from his plate of food as he prepared to savor that morsel before continuing his meal. But such delicacy was in keeping with his character—he was wise and gentle, and very intelligent, with a remarkable memory for people, whom he recognized by voice as well as by appearance, even those he had not seen for many years. Not many people could do as well. We believe animals to be lesser than ourselves but that is because we do not know them. By allowing us to know at least one of his kind, Christopher did us a great service.

"He lies in a grave in Hancock, near the barn that was his home."

THIS LETTER RAN IN THE TWO LOCAL WEEKLIES—PAPERS THAT had carried the news of Christopher's trespassings in their police logs in his younger days.

One of the papers didn't stop there. Alerted by Liz's letter, our friend, the *Monadnock Ledger*'s editor and novelist Jane Eklund, realized that Chris's death—and life—was news. The next day she came over, bearing a Mexican lasagna for dinner, to interview Howard and me for a longer article.

It ran as the lead story on the front page, complete with his photo—poking his great head through an oversized picture frame Howard had found at the dump, the pose from our latest Christmas card. "Christopher H: A Life Well Lived," read the banner headline. "Famous Pig Laid to Rest."

But by the time the papers came out, many people, both in town and beyond, already knew.

After I called my three closest women friends, I was able to speak to only a handful of others the day of Chris's death. I phoned Jarvis and Bobbie, and not only because they had been such good friends to Christopher; they would surely wonder what a backhoe was doing in the barnyard. I called Fiddle-heads to stop the flow of slops. I called Gary. I could not bring myself to speak to anyone else. I asked Gretchen to call George and Mary; Liz promised to tell our vet, Chuck, and his staff.

But word spreads fast in a small town. The news was on everyone's lips, from the Cash Market to Fiddleheads to Roy's grocery in Peterborough, where the image of Chris on his Christmas card was posted behind the meat counter.

The phone rang and rang. The answering machine over-flowed: "I'm so sorry." "I can't believe it." "He was really special." "Let me know what I can do." "He really was some pig!" To notify our out-of-town friends, Howard and I e-mailed Liz's beautiful tribute.

A classmate who had lived all of his life in cities and who now worked as a magazine editor in New York called to tell us, with great sincerity: "Of all the pigs I've known, yours was the coolest."

Cards and e-mails poured in. A producer from the public radio station, where so often our pig had been mentioned on the classical music program, sent my favorite pig quote, from Dylan Thomas: "The sunny slow lulling afternoon yawns and moons through the dozy town . . . Pigs grunt in a wet wallow-bath, and smile as they snort and dream. They dream of the acorned swill of the world, the rooting for pig-fruit." And this was her wish: "May Christopher always be dreaming of the acorned swill of the world."

In their condolences, people recounted their memories: "We remember the piglet who escaped from your hands, dragging his leash, and ran into the horse pasture in search of delectable apples," my literary agent from New York recalled from the first time she and her husband had come up to visit. "And Steve had to jump over the wooden fence to save him from the horses, who were very territorial. . . ."

"We have an indelible image," wrote Eleanor and Dick Amidon. "A misty morning and two pointed ears coming up the driveway through the mist, headed straight to the new lettuce. . . ."

"I can't believe how much I am feeling," Mollie wrote. "No more slops feeding, washings, cajoling him back into his pen with chocolate doughnuts. . . ."

"If there was ever wondering about Hog Heaven," wrote the postmistress, Pat, "Chris created it with everyone he saw. He is a legend and will go into the Hancock history books as the activist who brought people together with his beautiful love."

Christopher's influence, in fact, extended far beyond Hancock. Another college friend wrote from New York about how much Chris had meant to her young son, even though they had never met: "How sad that Stephen knows Christopher only from pictures. But please be assured, he is a true character in Stephen's life—as real as the boa constrictor his aunt saved from a careless pet owner who didn't realize the snake would get that big, and far more real than Piglet and Edward Bear and Rabbit in his storybooks. Stephen loves animals, and we love to tell animal stories to him just as he is drifting off to sleep. Christopher Hogwood was remarkable material for his bedtime ritual, but always with the promise they would meet someday. So Christopher Hogwood has taught us yet another lesson in his passing—stay close to your friends because, although they may seem endless, tomorows are finite."

And Girindra, through our translator the schoolteacher, wrote me from India: "I came to know the death news of Christopher; it could live more as you have been nursing it warmly but its day were numbered, so the God called it to him in the heaven. Your dear Christopher's death is a very painful shock to us, but as death is eternal and all soul use to rest in heaven, the pig should reach there leaving his old torn earthly body. May God bless him; he is a holy soul. I pray to Almighty for him. In this respect I shall say that you are the lucky one as you have served your best for relieving him. Who can do much more than this? It's a great satisfaction."

Just like when a person dies, people brought food, for food is life. Rice and lentils from Liz's daughter-in-law, Heather. The Mexican lasagna from Jane. Eleanor Briggs brought asparagus from her garden, as well as a nosegay of violets. Bobbie brought brownies—and so did Mary Garland, whose freezer, more than any other, had forever spoiled Chris's appetite for ordinary slops after the ice storm of '98. Chris would have approved.

Flowers flooded the house. As people once brought Chris their frost-killed autumn vegetables, now they brought cuttings from their spring gardens: tulips, lilacs, pansies. The Lillas sent a dozen red roses. We filled every vase and then all of the pickle jars. An orange hibiscus the size of a cruise missile arrived from my mother's friend, Scott Marchand, in Virginia. The publisher of my children's books sent a huge bouquet. Gary sent a cherry tree. His assistant, who knew Christopher only from Christmas cards, sent two huge pink flowering astilbes. Beth, the sole victim of Christopher's tusks, left a potted bleeding heart on the front step. I wondered if she remembered its bloody significance.

There were tributes both private and public. The capital city's daily, the *Concord Monitor,* reran the *Ledger*'s article about Chris as the lead story of the metro section in its Sunday edition. The original Christopher Hogwood, the famous conductor and musicologist for whom our pig was named, reran the obit on his official Web page. A local runner proposed to name an annual footrace after Christopher. Another friend arranged for a traditional Native American pipe and prayer ceremony to ease Christopher's transit to the next world. The fire department, whose members had retrieved him from his breakouts in his younger days, paid tribute on their marquee. Along with learning the weekly fire index—a blue, rainy 2 on a scale up to a flammable red 5—everyone who drove past the firehouse read the sign:

CHRISTOPHER HOGWOOD
RIP, ONE SPLENDID PIG!

Next door, Jarvis built a little bench at the edge of their backyard lawn, down by Moose Brook, and installed on it a small plaque. It read:

IN MEMORY OF CHRISTOPHER HOGWOOD
A GOOD NEIGHBOR AND PIG

The Miller-Rodats discussed whether they should drive up from Cambridge to make a monument to their friend. Maybe the boys could carve or build something for Christopher's grave, Mollie suggested. But Jack had a different idea:

"We should dig a huge hole, like Christopher used to dig," he said. "But leave a big hole there. A hole like he used to dig. A hole like in everybody's lives."

The hole in my heart was gaping. Howard was stronger than I. Now he fed the hens in the morning for me; he knew I couldn't go near the barn without falling apart, and unlike the times I had taken my sorrows to Christopher's stall and wept, now crying didn't make me feel better. My friends promised that time would help.

The bouquets dropped their petals. The new plants took root over Christopher's grave. A little more than a week after his death, Kate came home from college in Arizona and drove up with Lilla from Connecticut to say good-bye to Chris. Jane, in college in Colorado, would have come, too, but she was on a trip with a classmate's family.

I had saved all the petals from the flowers. Kate, Lilla, and I took the bowl of petals with us as we went out to the barnyard. Christopher's fresh grave was like a raw wound that love had tried to bandage with all those pretty plants. George, too, had come by, the day after Chris's death, bearing a pot of low-growing phlox and a small clay figurine of a smiling pig. The little statue served as a headstone. So now, as Kate, Lilla, and I knelt by the grave, we found ourselves together once again by the barn, looking into the face of a smiling pig.

Lilla took a handful of petals from the bowl.

"Thank you for the love grunts," she said, and placed some petals on the grave, like an offering.

Kate did the same. "Thank you for being, sometimes, my only friend."

"Thank you for laughing at us," I said.

And we continued, until all of the petals were gone:

"Thank you for eating all those slops."

"Thank you for your beautiful, soft ears."

"Thank you for digging great holes."

"Thank you for Pig Spa."

"Thank you for your great soul—for that gaze into our hearts."

"Thank you for all the friends you brought me."

"Thank you for loving all those days in the sun."

"Thank you for showing us your heart—for inviting us into such a happy heart."

SINCE THEN, I'VE HAD MANY MONTHS TO PONDER THE GIFTS THAT Christopher Hogwood, a runt pig who started out almost too small to live, had bestowed on those of us who knew him. Of course I had loved him; the fact that he was an animal was not a barrier to me, but a bridge. But what was it about this life that touched so many others so deeply?

His appeal was easy to see. He was adorable as a baby, and then delightful because he was so huge. Bringing him slops appealed to the Yankee sense of thrift; bringing him children made memories that would last kids a lifetime. People loved him because he was so happy. People loved him because he was so greedy. People loved him because he was so porcine—and people loved him because he was so human. Folks loved his gentleness and humor. But for many of his friends, it ran far deeper than that, as I found out in the months after his death.

THE REVELATIONS BEGAN WITH BOBBIE AND JARVIS.

A few weeks after Christopher's death, I went over to their house to talk. It was more than a social visit. Kate came with me. As a summer independent study for college, Kate was acting as my assistant as I began to research this book. We came back to the Doll House to record our neighbors' recollections of Christopher. And then talk turned to Bobbie and Jarvis's own pigs.

"I really loved those pigs," Bobbie told me and Kate, "and so did our boys." She remembered how their middle son used to come home from his first job after college and sit in the pigpen and have a soda with them after work. Bobbie remembered saying to her friends in upstate New York, " 'I don't know how I am going to stand it when these pigs go to market. I am so attached to them!' And they would say, 'You know, Bobbie, you have to be practical, they can't go through the winter.' And I believed them.

"So the day came in the fall when they were going to be picked up by the man who would execute them," Bobbie continued, "and I was going to work. And I said to Jarvis, 'I want them picked up before I come home, because I just can't stand it, and I don't want to see them go.' " But that fall day was rainy. The butcher's truck got stuck in their long, muddy driveway. When Bobbie came home, the butcher's truck still was there. She could hear the pigs squealing as they were pushed into the truck that would take them to be slaughtered.

"The reason I tell you this," she said to me and Kate, "is that it was so wonderful to come here and find Christopher. I have always been upset over those pigs." That's why it was so deeply satisfying, so healing for Bobbie and Jarvis to know Christopher. This is why the words of St. Francis had such special resonance at our barn. "Here was a pig that didn't have to go to market," said Bobbie. "Here was a pig that did live through the winter. It just made me feel so happy that I could be friends with a pig and nobody was ever going to take him away. That he was going to live a good long life and die a natural death. Which he did. It helped a lot."

As her words helped me.

Kate and I also interviewed Gretchen for her recollections. After we admired her new colt and petted her two mares, we sat on her couch with three Labradors and four cats and reminisced about Christopher. It was then that, for the first time, I heard the story of the Last Pig.

Long before I'd met Gretchen, back when her black hair hung to her waist and she lived in a solar-heated geodesic dome with her first husband, she used to raise pigs every year for meat. "It was back in the '70s, in the days when homesteading was in fashion," she said. "I cured my own ham. I made my own head cheese. I made my own scrapple." Each spring she'd get a couple of baby pigs. She'd give them good lives. She even gave each a six-pack of beer on their last day, so they'd be drunk before the butcher—amazingly, he was named Mr. Blood—came to shoot them. "But I never much thought about the pigs," she confessed—until one year, she acquired two little pink females. One of them was special.

This piglet leaped out of her pen regularly. At the age of three months, she could clear four feet. Normally, a loose pig on a farm is quite a nuisance, but not this pig. She liked to hang out with Gretchen as she gardened and tended her horses. The pig was good company. Sometimes she was helpful. One day, as Gretchen was struggling to empty a heavy bag of horse manure into the garden, the pig grabbed the other end in her mouth at just the right moment to help her disgorge its contents. Only once did the little pig root up part of the lawn. Gretchen had gone inside the house, and when she came out, she had to tamp the sod back down. "I said, 'No, we don't do that,' and put the sod back—and she never, ever, ever rooted again."

Gretchen's stepchildren grew to love this pig as well. When she got big enough, the kids used to ride on her as she walked around. Eventually, she was loose all the time. She stayed on the farm even if the family had to leave on some errand, and when they came back, the pig, who had learned the sound of the car, would run up and greet them, happy as a dog for the reunion.

Summer turned to fall, and the day came that the pigs would be killed. But Gretchen wanted to spare this pig. She would make a great breeder sow, she decided; she would keep her.

"So Mr. Blood pulls into the driveway," Gretchen told us, "and he has his .22, and of course the pig runs up to greet him like she did everyone else. And he said to me, 'Is this one of them?' And I said, 'Yes, but—'

"And he shot her in front of me."

She never raised another pig. But she loved it that Christopher had come to live with us, and she felt that his life fulfilled an important purpose.

"Christopher's death," Gretchen told me, "was the circle closing—the completion of a contract you had together." My life with him, Gretchen said, was the domestic parallel to my work overseas, writing about jungles and exotic species and indigenous peoples, finding models of how animals and people can live together in the world. But beyond that, she said, Chris and I had entered into what she considered a cosmic pact: "His coming to you, and your loving him, was a counterbalance, in a way, to the world's mistreatment of pigs," she said.

Gretchen does not feel that homestead farming is wrong; many animals live good lives on family farms. The cruelty happens on giant, crowded "factory farms," where living animals are treated like industrial products, and where 80 percent of America's sixty million pigs are raised for slaughter each year. "Of course, Christopher's story doesn't cancel out all the horrors pigs have suffered all over the world for so many centuries," Gretchen admitted. "But you and Chris created a different reality: of honoring a pig's life for the length of his natural life."

It was a reality that gave hope and peace in more ways than I could then imagine. For I had not yet spoken to my pastor, Graham, after Christopher's death.

Actually, Graham wasn't my pastor anymore. Much had happened since the early days at fellowship, when Graham would introduce me to new members by announcing I lived with a pig. The month after my father had died, Graham's wife, my friend Maggie, had been diagnosed with lung cancer. She died the following April. Since then, Graham had left our church, having been called to a new congregation. He is now happily remarried to a beautiful and accomplished art professor with three wonderful, now-grown children—all of whom, when they were smaller, came to know and love Christopher, bringing him slops and marveling at his size and gentleness and the spectacle of his greedy joy.

But Maggie's relationship with Chris had had a special intensity. It was not until thirteen years after her death, and a month after Christopher's, that I found out why.

"Didn't Maggie ever tell you about her childhood?" Graham asked.

She never had. Graham was surprised, given all the time we had spent together. When she was sick, I'd phoned her every day; near the end, I'd visited her in the hospital most days, often for hours. But we didn't talk about her past. Nor did we speak about her cancer. Mostly, we spoke of places we had traveled, animals we had known, and especially Christopher: what he had eaten, who had come to Pig Spa, tales of the latest escapes. I sent Maggie funny cards, usually picturing animals, and signed them from Christopher Hogwood. And she sent us cards equally funny, sweet animal cards, addressed to Chris.

"There's a reason she sent all those cards," Graham said. Her kindness was rooted in almost unimaginable tragedy.

Maggie's mother had gotten sick with cancer almost the moment Maggie was born—a situation for which she felt responsible. Her mother had died when Maggie was five. Her father, bereaved, became a vicious drunk. When Maggie was nine, her father killed himself with a revolver. Her older brother, twelve, found him dying on the bed, twitching.

The orphaned siblings were soon separated. When their father had been angry with them, he used to threaten: "I'll send you off to live with Aunt Frances!"—their mother's strict sister in Bangor, Maine. And this is what happened to Maggie. Aunt Frances didn't want Maggie, and she and her husband certainly weren't going to take Maggie's brother, too. So her brother was sent away to live with their father's brother in a different city.

I'd known Maggie was raised by her aunt, but not how awful it was—nor that her brother, a pharmacist, had become an alcoholic and committed suicide himself at age forty-one.

"Well, that's typical, never to talk about it," said Graham. "But I think there was a connection between all that and Christopher." He paused as I tried to imagine what connection there could be.

"Christopher was an orphan, too," he said. "But he was adopted by a very different family. He had a very different life. She sent him cards because when she was a little girl, nobody sent her cards. In other words, Christopher's story was her story—but come out right." In the life of this little runty piglet, Maggie could see her own story rewritten—transformed to a story of comfort and joy, a story with a happy ending.

. . .

CHRISTOPHER HOGWOOD, LILLA SAID TO ME SHORTLY AFTER HE died, "was a big Buddha master for us. He taught us how to love. How to love what life gives you—to love your slops. What a soul!" she said. "He was a being of pure love."

It's true. He loved company. He loved good food. He loved the warm summer sun, the belly rubs from caressing little hands. He loved this life. "That love," Lilla promised me, "is not lost. It can never be lost."

Christopher Hogwood knew how to relish the juicy savor of this fragrant, abundant, sweet, green world. To show us this would have been gift enough. But he showed us another truth as well. That a pig did not become bacon but lived fourteen years, pampered and adored till the day he died peacefully in his sleep—that's proof that we need not "be practical" all the time. We need not accept the rules that our society or species, family or fate seem to have written for us. We can choose a new way. We have the power to transform a story of sorrow into a story of healing. We can choose life over death. We can let love lead us home.

At the moment, the Pig Palace stands empty. People ask, "Will you get another pig?" This I don't know. But one thing I know for sure: a great soul can appear among us at any time, in the form of any creature. I'm keeping my eyes open.

Acknowledgments

Many of the people and animals who helped me with this book appear in these pages, where I hope my gratitude is evident. A number of others are not mentioned by name, even though their kindness to us and to our pig mattered deeply, and in many cases their recollections importantly informed these pages. These good souls are too numerous to name, but nonetheless I wish to thank them here.

Quite a number of people generously read this manuscript from its very earliest stages, offered encouragement, and made crucial suggestions. I am extremely lucky that some of my favorite writers number among those who agreed to do so: the splendid memoirist Beth Kephart; the poet Howard Nelson; my mentor, Elizabeth Marshall Thomas; the wonderful author Brenda Petersen; and my favorite writer of all time, Howard Mansfield. I am also grateful for the careful eyes and enduring friendship of Selinda Chiquoine, Joel Glick, Rob Matz, and Gretchen Vogel. My literary agent, Sarah Jane Freymann, has been a close friend of mine for many years and, of course, knew Christopher as well. Her advice and encouragement on this project were, as always, essential. I am grateful to my fine editor at Random House, Susanna Porter, who knows the joys of the animal world through her pet snails, beta, and three turtles; and to her talented assistant, Johanna Bowman, whose e-mails are often enlivened with attached pictures of mandrills, red river hogs, or tree kangaroos.

Finally, this book owes much to the efforts of my friend

and literary assistant, Kate Cabot. As this project began, she helped me conduct and transcribe a number of interviews. She interviewed Howard for this book, and also compiled archival research for me as part of an independent study project for Prescott College. It is she who titled this book. Thanks to Kate's excellent work, detailed recollections, and soothing presence here in the painful weeks after our pig's death, my heart was opened once again to Christopher's joyous spirit.

Sy Montgomery is a naturalist, author, documentary script-writer, and radio commentator who writes for children as well as adults. Among her award-winning books are *Journey of the Pink Dolphins, Spell of the Tiger,* and *Search for the Golden Moon Bear.* She has made four trips to Peru and Brazil to study the pink dolphins of the Amazon. On other expeditions she has been chased by an angry silverback gorilla in Zaire, bitten by a vampire bat in Costa Rica, undressed by an orangutan in Borneo, and hunted by a tiger in India. She has also worked in a pit crawling with eighteen thousand snakes in Manitoba, handled a wild tarantula in French Guiana, and swum with piranhas, electric eels, and dolphins in the Amazon. She lives in New Hampshire.

ABOUT THE TYPE

This book was set in Granjon, a modern recutting of a typeface produced under the direction of George W. Jones, who based Granjon's design upon the letter forms of Claude Garamond (1480–1561). The name was given to the typeface as a tribute to the typographic designer Robert Granjon.